I0822098

PATH TO A LONELY WAR

PATH TO A LONELY WAR

A Naval Hospital Corpsman with the Marines in Vietnam, 1965

Richard W. Schaefer

Texas Tech University Press

This book is typeset in Monotype Waldbaum. The paper used in this book meets the minimum requirements of ANSI/NISO Z39.48-1992 (R1997). ♾

Designed by Barbara Werden
Cover photograph/illustration by Tim Page

Library of Congress Cataloging-in-Publication Data

Names: Schaefer, Richard W., author.
Title: Path to a lonely war : a naval hospital corpsman with the Marines in Vietnam, 1965 / Richard W. Schaefer.
Description: Lubbock, Tex. : Texas Tech University Press, [2017] | Includes index.
Identifiers: LCCN 2017028130 (print) | LCCN 2017039911 (ebook) | ISBN 9781682830055 (ebook) | ISBN 9781682830024 (hardcover : alk. paper)
Subjects: LCSH: Schaefer, Richard W. | Vietnam War, 1961-1975—Medical care. | United States. Marine Corps. Marine Regiment, 4th. Battalion, 2nd. Company E—Biography. | United States. Navy—Hospital corpsmen—Biography.
| United States. Marine Corps—Hospital corpsmen—Biography. | Vietnam War, 1961-1975—Personal narratives, American.
Classification: LCC DS559.44 (ebook) | LCC DS559.44 .S34 2017 (print) | DDC 959.704/37—dc23
LC record available at https://lccn.loc.gov/2017028130

Printed in the United States
17 18 19 20 21 22 23 24 25 / 9 8 7 6 5 4 3 2 1

Texas Tech University Press | Box 41037
Lubbock, Texas 79409-1037 USA | 800.832.4042
ttup@ttu.edu | www.ttupress.org

This book is dedicated to all those people and their families who left a part of themselves and a piece of their heart in South Vietnam.

To my wonderful, young grandsons, Harvey and Jett . . . peace always.

CONTENTS

ILLUSTRATIONS

ACKNOWLEDGMENTS

As I looked ahead they were always there in front of me on the trail. They would be the first to confront an elusive and dangerous enemy. It was their job. They were the ones who manned the guard posts around our perimeter, protecting me while I slept. They were also the ones who brought in the food, water, and mail, and yes, they were also the ones who dug the latrines. All of these things and more was their job, and they wouldn't have it any other way.

Sometimes it appeared as if the lower ranks were treated roughly by their sergeants. Over time I realized that they were being treated as professional equals. They were all marines, and they were treated as men who were supposed to know their jobs and who would do their best no matter what. Rank had nothing to do with it. This was the expectation and the mutual understanding they signed on for in becoming a Marine. Their mutual survival depended on it.

Marines didn't bestow many accolades to their rank and file. It wasn't because they didn't deserve the recognition. I saw firsthand that they did. I think it was that being marines they were supposed to outperform. Being a Marine was enough. That is theirs to hold dear for the rest of their lives. I am very proud to have served with them, and I publicly say, "Thank you!" to the US Marine Corps for allowing me to walk the many miles alongside your men as we accomplished our mission as one.

PATH TO A LONELY WAR

INTRODUCTION

Somewhere between the "greatest generation" and the all-volunteer armed forces of today were those of us who either volunteered for or were drafted into military service. As a result, many of us found ourselves participating in a lengthy war effort in South Vietnam that many people came to hate, and few would support. Never before in our history have troops returning home been spat on or referred to as "baby killers," while countless good citizens of the "silent majority" stood by and did little or nothing to express their opinion one way or the other, let alone convey their gratitude for the job those returning had done.

As memory allows, the following words either tumbled or had to be summoned out of the cobwebbed archives of my mind. Sometimes they were derived from the memories of an older man, and at other times were seen through the eyes of an older boy on his way to becoming a young man. Perhaps it is when these two sets of recollections and images intersect, the more interesting thoughts are conveyed. Hopefully the reader will think so, too, and enjoy following along with me on my short and occasionally eventful military call to duty as a naval hospital corpsman attached to a US Marine Corps infantry battalion for more than three years.

Only recently, and after I had written my manuscript, our local newspaper began a series of articles under the heading, *Vietnam: 50 Years Later, Serving with Honor*. Each day for fifty days the paper featured an area veteran talking about his or her service and time in the military during the Vietnam War. At about the halfway mark of their publication, the editor of the paper wrote that the response to the series was overwhelming. The newspaper's readers responded positively to these stories unlike anything the editors anticipated or had experienced. The newspaper has a print circulation of approximately forty thousand in addition to its online and social media presence.

From this feedback in the newspaper and on the Internet I had the impression that the readers were genuinely eager to learn about the veterans' individual experiences and impressions of the Vietnam War. In addition the newspaper released short videos of them describing their feelings and sentiments to the reporter. Their explanations of what went on during those times were unique unto themselves, yet similar in many of their interpretations and conclusions about their military service and duty to country. The majority of these individuals said that they joined the military service to avoid being drafted. They wanted to choose the time and branch of military service as well as get their obligation to serve over and done. Some of them strongly believed that they would be stationed in South Vietnam. Some didn't mind going overseas, but some of them did. It was definitely a factor in their decision-making process regarding which branch of service and the time to enlist. In my case I do not remember being aware in 1962 that we had a military involvement in South Vietnam that could affect me. It was certainly not in the news every day or discussed in high school. Three years would pass before large numbers of combat forces landed in South Vietnam.

Many of the subjects of the newspaper's stories wished that the generals could have had more influence on the military decisions in Vietnam. They thought that the significant influence of politics hindered military progress. Nearly all of those interviewed expressed the belief that our primary goal was to help the South Vietnamese people defend themselves against the communist insurgents and North Vietnamese military. Many of those interviewed still believe this to be true. A significant percentage of the veterans were affected directly by antiwar demonstrators as they returned home. All of them appear to have understood why there were demonstrations against the war, but none of them understood why they were spat on and shunned. As with previous wars' veterans, those from Vietnam presumed that other Americans would be glad they were coming home. Some returning from Vietnam were advised not to wear their military uniform in public even as they were traveling home. These examples are but a sampling of comparable experiences.

Reading about their impressions and the impact on their postmilitary lives pleased me such that I decided to overcome my initial thoughts on writing the following narrative. Before working on the manuscript, I had concluded that very few people really cared about Vietnam anymore. *That's old news*, I thought. Maybe so, but this newspaper series certainly touched a nerve. I personally gained a reintroduced sense of pride in what the United States attempted to do in Southeast Asia. Militarily we were on the same page regarding our mission and obligation, and I was not surprised at the positive attitude toward duty. Our own country, however, was not always on the same page, which is one of many reasons the Vietnam War was such a galvanizing historical event.

I started writing this account for a variety of reasons. I wanted to help squelch the notion that our military at the time was not up to standard or that we were not mentally as tough as service members in previous wars. The best way for me to do so was to demonstrate by example how we performed our duties and met our commitments in an honorable manner. Not all of the troops in South Vietnam were smoking pot, undisciplined, or unaccomplished in fulfillment of their duties. Hollywood, the press, and some works that would have been better unpublished frequently characterized the troops in such a manner. Primarily I want the reader to gain further insight and depth of understanding from someone with ground-level, hands-on experience concerning war, Vietnam, and the sacrifices made by all involved.

From a personal standpoint I wrote this narrative because I wanted something for my grandchildren to have in order to learn more about their grandfather's life in the days before they knew him. In addition, I wanted something for my immediate family, even though they have heard me speak about Vietnam and other military experiences. My genuine desire is for the book to function as a human-interest story. I do not consider this a war story but one that describes what happened to a particular young man and many like him. I would feel privileged if veterans and active-duty military personnel were among an interested readership. Veterans could perhaps contrast their experiences during their military service to mine, and active-duty men and women could possibly have a better idea of what they may face in the not-so-distant future.

Path to a Lonely War is about a trek that was only the beginning for me, as I had just recently graduated high school. I wanted very much to prove to my family, friends, and relatives; the community at large; and myself that I could make the right decisions and make it on my own. They were the ones who meant the most to me at this particular juncture in my life, and I highly valued their thoughts and opinions. Over the next four years I would have ample opportunity to self-examine and evaluate my progress as I stepped out of my secure environment to conquer the world. I invite the reader to look back with me at the four-year path I took to a lonely war and back home again, returning as a different person than when I left.

I use the phrase "lonely war" not to depict sadness but instead to describe the isolation that some of us serving in Vietnam felt. The war was contentious, eventually dividing the country not only in terms of support for the conflict itself but also in terms of directly blaming the troops for our overall situation at home and abroad. From almost the beginning to the very end of our involvement, the antiwar movement grew, and so did the perception by many in the military that the country had turned its back on them.

I have an article from *US News & World Report* dated November 1965 that my mother clipped for me that included letters from an array of military rank and file voicing their dissatisfaction regarding the protests. I wrote a note to my hometown newspaper in Nebraska in December of that same year commenting on the war protests. Yes, we all noticed. In my opinion, our country took a path from mild support to almost no support for the war. Moreover, the people lost faith in the nation's military, which I think propelled the sense of a lonely war. The antiwar demonstrations and protests, even if not intended to in most cases, provided our enemy with yet another source of propaganda to use against us.

All of our lives we are taught from an early age at home, at school, and from our faith tradition that it's wrong to harm, let alone kill someone. In a combat situation the rules are turned upside down. The expectations are to do exactly what we know is wrong—a very heavy emotional

A Letter From Richard Schaefer In Viet Nam

Chu Lai, South Viet Nam
8 December 1965

Dear Mr. and Mrs. Payne and Family

I want to thank all Hooperites and especially Gwen Knigge of Fremont for your wonderful letter to me in the December 2nd issue.

Many of us here feel a little ashamed of the people who protest and demonstrate the effort in Viet Nam. We also realize that they are a small minority who are probably insecure, and the non-tninkers who just want to be heard.

I'll always know that our efforts here are not in vain because of people like there are in Hooper, Nebraska, U. S.A. I hope to see many of you next year.

Sincerely yours,
R. W. Schaefer HM3
2nd Battalion 4th Marines
H & S Co. (Medical Section)
c-o F. P. O. San Francisco, Calif.

P. S. I hope Mrs. Osterloh will foregive my grammar.

(Editor's Note . . Richard, there is nothing wrong with your grammar . . it is perfect. We just left the P. S. on because we knew it would please Mrs. Osterloh. All our affectionate wishes for a Happy New Year, and PEACE.)

Intro. 1. I wrote this letter to the publishers of the town newspaper and the people back home expressing my sentiments about the protests. Courtesy of *Hooper* (NE) *Sentinel*, presently the *Rustler Sentinel* (Hooper, Nebraska).

adjustment to make on an individual basis, maybe one of the most difficult to accept and simply move on. Going through such situations affects everybody in one way or another. In some cases it shows right away, and in others it takes a while. For a certain segment, nothing ever seems evident or comes to the surface, which is perhaps the saddest testament to the ancillary effects of war.

ONE

Three Boys in the Back

I was born and reared in Marysville, Kansas, then and now a small county-seat farm town, tucked away in the low, rolling flint hills of northeast Kansas. Farmland, meandering creeks, and deciduous timber dot the countryside, intertwined with the rocky grasslands that Pony Express riders valiantly galloped over decades earlier. The lay of the land was not at all like the image of Kansas so often portrayed as the flat, immense, treeless wheat field of *The Wizard of Oz*. My town with the pretty-sounding name was home to independent, hard-working people from all walks of life, but primarily it supported the surrounding agricultural community that in turn provided the town's life's blood.

Marysville was also something of a railroad town, with trains passing directly through the downtown area, including its main street, many times in a given day. The Pacific Hotel had a large coffee shop on the main floor, and down the street was a beautiful depot for boarding and getting off the train. Little did anyone know it then, but these unique-looking passenger cars were to become a thing of the past in Marysville. Progress is often difficult to recognize as it is taking place, while history captures some of the things we see but don't necessarily notice every day. Today the railroad tracks have been relocated so that the many trains that still pass skirt along the edge of town under a large overpass, but the depot is being restored to its original beauty.

In this small town I formed some of the rudiments of my character and dreamed what my future might entail. I was the eldest of four children, each two years apart, who all managed to keep both parents fully busy, working, and otherwise making ends meet for a family of six. My two brothers, our baby sister, and I relied on Mom as the go-to person of the family who held it all in control. She made sure that everybody had clean and freshly ironed clothes along with satisfactorily filled lunch boxes during the school year. Mom also maintained a clean and orderly house, baked excellent breads and pies, and saw to it that we always had good solid meals, especially for supper, where the whole family gathered together each night.

At the table, all of us learned of the trials and tribulations of the day's events, and even if things were not always great, a positive look forward was where the discussions normally ended. Sometimes we were catching Dad up on what the rest of us already knew from getting home earlier in the day. When he asked one of us kids, "What's wrong?" no one had the luxury of looking down and saying, "Nothing much." If it was personal and not for general discussion, he made sure to have a later discussion with whoever was having problems. No one was made to feel all alone. Even if one of us wanted to solve our own problems, we could still count on involvement from Mom and Dad. Airing out a particular issue rather than have it fester unattended usually helped, even though it sure didn't seem like it at times.

Dad didn't go to parent-teacher conferences, but he looked at every report card to examine the grades and the teachers' progress remarks. One of the family's cardinal rules was that there would be no discipline issues at school. If a note was ever sent home regarding behavior or a lack of respect for the teachers, the results would be devastating to the posterior portion of the guilty party's anatomy. On the other hand, if any teacher had ever laid a hand on, or taken a paddle to, any of his kids, Dad would have gone to school and had a discussion with the teacher. He could have done whatever was necessary, but it never came down to it. None of us wanted any part of the embarrassment his visit would bring upon us at school.

Nearly every year in the summer we would all pack up the family car and go on a road trip out of state. The three boys sat in the back, and little sister was up front between Mom and Dad. This same arrangement held for every trip, whether going downtown or on vacation. We made repeated trips some seven hundred miles to Minnesota for camping, swimming, and fishing. We ventured west over the Rocky Mountains to Washington and stopped in Yellowstone Park. All of the trips were made in one car as a family, and we normally camped out along the way. We could not afford motels and restaurants. I doubt that, until years later, any of us kids really appreciated the effort Mom and Dad put into these trips. I marvel at how in the world they packed all of our belongings into the trunk of the car and a car-top carrier, which was not much more than a couple of two-by-fours with suction cups and straps. It was not all singing and smiles—and there was no air conditioning—but we all did it together through the good and the bad times alike.

Dad worked at the local flour and animal feed mill for a number of years in a variety of positions, one of which was to drive the company truck delivering feed and large sacks of flour to the many smaller communities around the local area. Some of my fondest memories were when Dad invited me to help with the deliveries. Fifty-pound sacks of feed carried from the front to the back of the truck, then taken by a two-wheeled cart to the storage area, weren't so hard, but when it came to the hundred-pound burlap flour sacks, Dad took over. I observed with pride and learned from seeing how well my father interacted with the customers and other people we encountered throughout the day. Being my dad's number-one helper most certainly meant a hot roast beef sandwich and mashed potatoes smothered in dark brown gravy at one of the local cafés on the route. Of course, this was sometimes accompanied by a piece of pie and always an ice-cold bottle of soda pop.

Mostly these deliveries were opportunities to spend some time with my dad, just the two of us. Out of the corner of my eye I watched my father flick the ash dangling from his burning Camel cigarette out of the driver's-side window as he steered his truck down the bumpy, gravel-laden county roads. If the ash happened to fall short of the window and land on the floor, it didn't really matter, for it blended right in with the pieces of gravel and dirt from all over the county lying on the floor of the cab anyway. We talked about anything and sometimes nothing at all. In the bright Kansas sun we could see about ten miles away in any direction, which included the normally blue standpipes (water towers) with their respective town's names proudly painted on them. It was like the town was telling the world, "We're over here, please come see us." Dad knew all the roads and the town locations like the back of his hand, and he certainly didn't need these structures to tell which town was ahead or if their delivery schedule was being maintained.

When I wasn't helping Dad, my childhood and adolescent years were filled with Boy Scouts, fishing for whatever was biting in the Big Blue River and local creeks, hunting for anything that moved in the timber (normally rabbits and squirrels), and endless hours spent riding my bicycle over the county gravel roads and the brick-covered streets in town. As long as I was fishing along the river I occasionally explored the old junked cars placed along the bank for erosion control. There was always something of value in or on them, in my opinion. Once I found an emerald-green steering knob, which I removed from a steering wheel. For those who don't remember, a steering wheel knob is an attachment for a steering wheel that, when used correctly, can enable the driver to turn the steering wheel with only the knob, such as when making a U-turn or turning a corner. I proudly brought it home, only to find that Dad didn't want a "knuckle-buster" on his car's steering wheel. You can still buy steering wheel knobs, but Dad cautioned us to keep two hands on the wheel, which isn't a bad idea. My short-lived career as a picker hadn't even gotten off the ground floor.

I relished the times I spent hunting the timbers with my .22-caliber single-shot, then later with my semiautomatic rifle. I became a good marksman using the single-shot, but then I became a bit sloppy with the semiautomatic weapon. As the name implies, with the single-shot weapon, I only had one shot at the game before I had to reload, which often meant it was too late to get off another shot. With my semiautomatic all I had to do was squeeze the trigger each time for as many shells as I had loaded into it. Carrying a rifle meant a heavy responsibility for safety. All that was necessary to lose the privileges of hunting would have been to be careless or irresponsible one time. There was no three-strike rule in effect back then, at least in our house.

Frequently, my brothers and I would ride our bikes the ten miles or so to our grandparents (our mother's parents) farm just to say hi to them and our uncles and aunt, then we would turn back around and ride back home, stopping along the way for a pop and candy bar at the one and only country store in little Marietta, Kansas. We made sure that we had enough time to hurl a few rocks into the Big Blue River from the large, old metal and wooden plank bridge that took us safely from one side of the river to the other. None of us thought much about it then, but as we stopped periodically to take a break, we also were taking in the sights, sounds, and even the smells of what Mother Nature and the farmers working the land provided. Even today, the smell of freshly cut hay or soil being turned in the spring, or the sound of a turtledove calling its mate, all trigger fond memories from days many years ago.

I became an Eagle Scout at a very young age, and my mother was the one who made sure that I earned every one of the required merit badges, especially the hiking badge. These hikes were often routed along the highway where my brothers and I would collect and stash piles of pop bottles alongside the road in the ditch because they were worth two cents apiece to the local bottlers. It also helped with the litter problem. In those days, if it fit through the car or truck window, it landed in the ditch. After hikes of five, ten, and even twenty miles, Mom was the cab-driver, along with our little sister riding along, who picked up all the hikers and stopped multiple times to let us retrieve our treasures stored temporarily along the highway. Later everyone would help count the bottles and cash them in for spending money. Even with the Kansas sun relentlessly beating down on us, we didn't stop the hike and definitely didn't suspend our bottle collection. There weren't any cell phones to call home for an early pickup from softhearted Mom. Finishing the job in such conditions and not deviating from the planned arrangements would soon prove to be an asset for this young Kansan. Having the discipline to adhere to the rules laid out before the hikes, such as staying together and not venturing from the designated course, provided the basic tenets of honoring an agreed-upon set of conditions.

As a high school student I washed the storefront windows at the local J. C. Penney and Ben Franklin department stores after school, was a junior lifeguard, delivered advertising handbills on Saturdays, and worked as a hired hand for some of the area farmers, helping them with baling hay and other chores as needed. The farmers had a way of getting their dollar-per-hours' worth of work out of the hired help, but on the other hand, the farmers themselves also did everything that they asked us to do. The problem was that the farmers were usually bigger and stronger than the hired help, not to mention being much more knowledgeable about what needed to be done. This type of work might be classified as character building. My brothers and sister also had jobs either around the house or around town when they became old enough.

Money was always tight, and while Mom and Dad could be counted on for some occasional funds, we were expected to earn some if not most of what we needed for our spending. We also were expected to spend our hard-earned monies on sensible things we needed or wanted, not fritter it away on "junk," which was subject to parental opinion. When I was sixteen years old I purchased a boat from an adult coworker at the sheet metal shop where I worked summers. He described it to me as a small wooden rowboat that he hadn't used for a while. I could have it for twenty dollars, and it was stored in a corncrib about ten miles out of town.

All excited to tell my dad about this new purchase, I ran home with the big news. Dad, a brother-in-law of his who was visiting from New Mexico, and I drove out to bring the boat home. We located the corncrib, swung open its doors, and there the beauty was, high up in the rafters just like the man said. Dad went inside, and suddenly he began laughing and making a few uncomplimentary remarks about my new boat. The brother-in-law, who occasionally stuttered, said, "What's the matter, B-B-B-Butch?" to which Dad replied, "Hell, I built this boat years ago, used it, then got rid of it." It turned out to have a hole in it, was rotted out, and otherwise not worth anything. My uncle then turned and said, "Well, it looked good from out here by the door, didn't it, B-B-Big Boy?" and he and Dad both bent over laughing at my expense 'til their ribs ached. My coworker gave back the boat money a couple of days later because he didn't want to be accused of cheating a kid. He had obviously heard that my dad was not happy about it. Welcome to lessons in self-pride and humility!

As I was about to enter my senior year in high school, Dad decided to accept a new position with another firm selling feed and animal nutritional products in Nebraska, some 150 miles to the north. This was a traumatic event at the time, or so it seemed then, but in the end it worked out well. Although the little town of Hooper, Nebraska, was even smaller than my hometown in Kansas, the people in Nebraska were great, and the school system was very good. Here we begin this Kansan—soon to be Nebraskan—towhead's journey over the next four years, as I navigate my venturesome path toward manhood.

TWO

What Now, Young Man?

When we were kids, all that either one of my brothers had to say was "war," and off we would go to retrieve our small armies of men and weapons. Our armies were little plastic military or cowboy figures standing about three inches tall with flat horizontal bases under their boots for stability purposes. We "recruited" most of them from the local five-and-dime store. They could be positioned anywhere in the house. They were perched high in the cavernous "mountains" of the sofa arms and easy chairs, or maybe they would simply hide behind all of the excellent military structure found in the confines of our living room. The rules of war were simple. My brothers and I took turns firing on each other's army one shot at a time, unless of course a soldier was hit, then another shot was allowed.

The weapons could have been rubber bands pulled back over our fingers, aimed at a soldier, then released, but we had much more sophisticated weaponry at our disposal. Necessity as the mother of invention was fully deployed when we readied for battle. Our weapons of choice were small plastic missile launchers that could be loaded with their appropriate missiles then fired with the release of a small spring-loaded lever on the launcher. We took turns claiming them as prizes in breakfast cereal boxes, as I recall. There were several different types, such as Atlas, Nike, and others, available for collecting. These were the same models we would use against the Russians, should the need ever arise. Instead of launching the little missiles into "space," we aimed them like small guns, firing the missile at each other's men. My brothers and I eventually became skilled enough to launch them airborne in an arclike pattern so that the projectile could make a direct hit on the opposition. We didn't strategically analyze it then, but the inference could be made that the concept was similar to firing mortar rounds or artillery into the air. If the men fell over, they were taken out of commission. The winner was the one with the last man standing.

My brothers and I spent hours playing war. A more civil term would have been to say we were playing "army." Needless to say, we became quite adept at knocking off each other's forces and improving our strategy development skills. It was great fun back in those days, where it was all pretend. It's probably not politically correct these days to play such games. These were the days of six-shooters, pocket knives, cowboy hats, and violent cartoons, and we even played outside in all kinds of weather, making up our own games. Yes, we did have to make believe, and we did have to use our imagination at times.

It didn't hurt a thing because, you see, the cartoon characters always survived, and we didn't have any problem in distinguishing the good guys from the bad ones. The good guys always won, though. This was also true in almost all of the movies, which I think was a good message then and now.

I don't really know if we ever outgrew playing these games. I imagine that a collector of memorabilia would give more than pocket change for these toys in today's market. Our little sister probably could have beat all of us at this, but we seldom invited her to participate. She undoubtedly thought we were silly, but I think she would have liked to have been an army general once in a while, too. There was no excuse for our behavior except for bad manners on the part of my brothers and myself, and we were having too much fun with this ourselves.

It was 1962, a time right out of the 1973 movie *American Graffiti*, and school was out for the summer—or in my case, school was out and done. How many times can one person be asked, "What are you gonna do now that you're out of school?" How many times did I want to say, "*Nothing!*" Since time stands still for no one, I guess it was time to act like an adult, in as much as I was beginning to look the part. As a carry-over from the school year, many of the guys still scheduled their Friday afternoon haircuts to ensure that they would look good for the upcoming weekend. After all, a young stud never knew whom he might meet or how downright lucky with the girls he might get, although we had a pretty good idea that our luck was not going to change for the better.

In those days young men's hair styles were crew cut (short and uncombed), flattop (short and butch waxed straight up on the top, looking something like a lawn on Viagra), Ivy League (short with a perfect straight-line part on the right or left side of the head with the hair combed neatly across), fenders (flattop on top of the head and ducktails on the sides), and ducktails for the Elvis look. I think there was even a style called the Caesar, with the hair combed forward and evenly trimmed with bangs coming slightly down the forehead. These styles and a few others were on a large poster on the wall of the barber shop, establishing a credible link to the look one would have upon exit. It was also helpful for when a guy's dad might ask, "What in the hell kind of haircut is that?" because he too would have seen the same poster on the wall when he had his own ears lowered. It didn't matter that much when the latest hairstyle was altered, because the poster remained a fixture on the wall of the barbershop for all time. Many years later I noticed what appears to be the same poster on an episode of *The Andy Griffith Show*. There it was, hanging on the wall of Floyd's Barbershop, but that is as far as any similarities between the barbershops go. Ours was much more hip and up to date, of course.

The cars and hot rods cruising the main drag of town in the summer evenings looked cool, the kids were having fun, and the Nebraskaland farm girls looked pretty darned special, too. I didn't have a car of my own to cruise around town, but getting a ride with a buddy wasn't a big problem. Actually, my dad and I went in as equal partners on a 1930 Model A Coupe when we first moved to Nebraska. It was black with yellow wheels, and it was a cherry from a body perspective. Mechanically, the car had a few issues, but nothing to stop us from driving it the forty-five miles home when we bought it for two hundred dollars. We drove it in parades, and I agreed not to use it for riding aimlessly around town or transforming it into a street rod, as if I had the mechanical skills, knowledge, or money to do such a thing. Dad was an adept mechanic in his own right, and I believe he would have loved it if I would have had the interest and curiosity to try and work on the car, but I didn't except for replacing the interior cloth and keeping it waxed and shiny.

I had just graduated from high school and had made a lot of new friends for having only lived in Nebraska for a year. In those days, graduation from high school signaled that the time had come, and it was expected of us, to figure out what we were going to do next and where we were going to do it. Warranted or not, I felt pressured that I had to make decisions about the rest of my life and make them soon. The heat was on, perhaps more self-imposed than anything else, to initiate some action on my behalf. Attending college wasn't a certainty or even an expectation like it is today. It was the goal of many in my senior class, and a lot of them had the financial resources to pursue their educational objectives. Most of my fellow graduates were farm kids, whose families had good land to farm, and they were successful at it. The soil in this flat Nebraska valley was excellent for crop yields, and the weather didn't appear to bake everything during the summer as it sometimes did in Kansas.

My predicament was that I had few ideas, no real plans, and little money to do much of anything. Ordinarily there were three or four options for a young man right out of high school: attend college or trade school, sign up for military service, work on the family farm, or work somewhere—anywhere—other than your hometown. No way was I going to get a job and continue to live at home, unless I was in farming. That just didn't fit the perception of being out on your own to peers, or relatives for that matter. The goal was to strike out, take responsibility, be a man, earn some money, and maybe, just maybe, do something for the good of society. The Peace Corps may have been an option, but there wasn't much known about it at the time, at least locally.

These were the days of John F. Kennedy, after all. "Ask not what your country can do for you. Ask what you can do for your country." Being a male, I had one ominous shadow hanging over my head: the good ol' military draft ("Uncle Sam Wants You"). It wasn't that they wanted me now, but the message was that they would be seeing me sometime soon enough. At age eighteen I had to register with the draft board, and unless

I had a college deferment or some family hardship, it was likely that I would spend some time in uniform, sooner rather than later. My dad always told my siblings and me that these were the best days of our lives, and for us to enjoy them now, because they wouldn't last forever. It is still baffling to me how much smarter my parents became as I grew older. Maybe high school hadn't been so bad after all.

Being drafted typically meant service in the US Army for two years on active duty and four years in the reserves. Everyone had to complete a commitment of six years total in those days. The navy, Marine Corps, air force, and I believe the Coast Guard programs were four years active duty with two years of inactive reserve time. I could also enlist in the army or National Guard, or join other reserve programs in the other military branches with varying lengths of time commitments involved. If I signed up—enlisted—for active duty on my own, I got it over with at the time of my choosing and had my choice of the specific branch of the military that I "wanted" to be in. It boiled down to the following: Did I want to sail the high seas, be around planes, or pound mud? At least that was the picture engrained in my seventeen-year-old brain at the time. As it turns out, I wasn't that far off in my preliminary, adolescent assessment.

I had long thought that I had the desire to go on to college after high school, but in reality I may have liked the idea of going to college more than actually attending classes. It seemed that a sizeable number of my graduating classmates were going off to college or would be attending some type of trade school. While our family was not poor, there wasn't such money around for college expenses. No one in our entire family had ever attended college. I had two younger brothers and my sister still living at home, which meant that money was closely managed. That is the way it always had to be. One thing in our family almost above all else was that, as much as possible, each sibling was to have the same as the others in terms of whatever opportunity the family was able to assist with or provide. We had to earn that assistance by working hard and staying out of trouble, and we all wanted whatever was best for each other. There had always been competition in our family, but jealousy and selfishness were not often evident.

My parents were supportive in whatever I chose to do. One option not available to me was loafing around the house doing nothing. During the summer I discovered that the US Navy had a program in which if I enlisted before my eighteenth birthday, I would be released from active duty when I turned twenty-one years of age. This translated into a time commitment of only three years versus four years of active duty. I think they called it a "minority cruise," for lack of a better term.

Procrastination plagues me from time to time (and still does), so I did nothing regarding the military early on in the summer of my newfound freedom from high school. The only decision I made was that I was sure that I would not be enlisting in the army or Marine Corps. I believed that the navy offered more diversity regarding the types of jobs I would be doing. I understood this in part from what I had read and also heard concerning naval training possibilities. Some of my uncles on both my dad's and mom's sides of the family had served in the navy, which resulted in a slight historical bias toward this branch of military service.

The activities in South Vietnam were not really a part of this evaluation. As I mentioned earlier, I don't believe that I was—nor were many people in general—cognizant of what the US military commitments were then. The pressure on me to do something mounted when July came and I turned eighteen. I had missed the small window available to me concerning the three-year active-duty option. No one said anything about it, but I think my parents had wished that for my own sake I would have made up my mind by then.

The day did arrive when I came to the conclusion that I would not be attending college in the fall. I walked uptown to where there was a private-pay telephone, phoned the naval recruiter, and invited him to come to our home for a visit. When I returned home, Dad was outside in the yard working on the family car, and I told him that I was joining the navy. He looked sort of taken aback, then he asked me if I was sure of my decision. I told him that's what I intended to do, after which he paused, then said reluctantly, "Better go tell your mother," which I did, and she cried. I think my whole family was in disbelief over what I was doing, but they were all behind whatever I had decided to do. I was, after all, the first one of us to leave home, and it felt as though I were breaking up the family. I remember feeling good, but scared—but I had at least made a decision about my future.

Dad was never in the military due to his being sightless in his left eye because of a childhood accident. To look at my dad, one couldn't tell that he had such a handicap. He never let it stop him from doing all the things, such as hunting and fishing, that he enjoyed, and he certainly didn't let it stop him from working at any job that he ever had. Rumor was that there were some instances during World War II where some of the local guys back home commented to him in a less-than-complimentary tone about not being in the military. That was a big mistake for their small lapse in judgment, because my dad was quite able to defend himself physically, seeing only with his one good eye better than most men were able to do with two. I heard of a few times down at the local Saturday night dance that he quieted down some of the loudmouths who were brandishing a feeble degree of beer-bottle courage, which is when one gains courage commensurate with the amount of beer consumed. Dad had attempted to enlist in the military more than once, but there was no waiver, and he couldn't serve. He was sensitive about not serving, especially during the Second World War, but he had no reason to be ashamed of his medical issue either. I don't remember him ever complaining to my mother or to anyone else about having the use of only one eye, and he never used it as an excuse.

The recruiter didn't waste any time coming to our home shortly after I had phoned him. He presented his song-and-dance routine, and the day he visited I signed on with the US Navy. The only thing I knew for sure was that I would be going to San Diego, California, for boot camp/recruit training. After that I could go wherever the navy needed me. My hesitation in doing this before my eighteenth birthday resulted in my having to serve one additional year of active duty, which almost cost me a lot more than that, as becomes apparent later. On July 30, 1962, I found myself in Omaha, Nebraska, standing in a room full of naked men taking my physical examination and reciting my enlistment oath to my country (with my clothes on), and I eventually boarded a train for San Diego. The next eleven weeks of this new adventure would prove to be interesting and enlightening in a variety of ways. The trip to San Diego took a couple of days, with frequent stops along the way. I was beginning to see the world in an entirely different light already.

Each recruit had a private room on the train, which provided an opportunity to sit back and look out the window at this vast country we were skimming by, the country that I just signed up to officially serve for six long years. Listening to the repetitive sounds of the railcars passing over the tracks, and watching the sun disappear into the night, I already had the initial feelings of homesickness. The closer we got to San Diego, the more I had the feeling that I was heading off to jail, and that I had made a big mistake by signing up. *What in the hell did I get myself into?* My dad had an expression that he didn't use very often, but it got the point across. He would say, "What in *the* hell happened or what in *the* hell did you do?" The emphasis on the word *the* was usually a confirmation that the situation was serious, and it could also signal that there wasn't a damn thing he could do about it or to get me out of it. This time around I was the one asking this question. Evidently I wasn't the only recruit who felt this way. One guy in particular bragged that he was going to fake his way out of the navy once he was in San Diego. Damned if he didn't accomplish his goal some weeks later by sleepwalking or complaining of some other medical problem. My thought even back then was that later in his life he may come to regret his dereliction of duty.

In my own case I just kept the thought in the back of my mind that I was getting my military obligation out of the way, and that I would have plenty of time to live the life I really wanted to live once that duty was fulfilled. The only resentment that I harbored was that I wasn't totally on board with being forced to do something because of the military draft. It was not an absolute that I would be drafted, but the consensus at the time was that it was inevitable. This was the correct assumption as it turned out. During the peak manpower needs of the Vietnam War, they were even drafting into the Marine Corps. I wasn't thinking about duty to country or anything so noble at this point in my enlistment. The reality of being drafted was a formidable obstacle to deal with for an eighteen-year-old. It wasn't taught as a part of any school curriculum, and it should have been. The draft board wasn't interested in any voice of opposition, only in getting their quotas filled.

THREE

Heading West to Become a Man

Why is everyone yelling at us and calling us names all the time? I should have conducted a more in-depth analysis about what boot camp entailed, because I needed to board the learning-curve train in short order. They didn't explain things twice. I appreciated the military's objective, which was to transform us from a diverse and somewhat sorry lot of recruits into a uniform group capable of functioning as one unit. If yelling at you day and night was a means to success, then we were about to become the most successful naval recruiting class San Diego had ever processed. I had my doubts then, as I do now, that constantly being told that we were as worthless as dog doo was the optimum way to instill confidence. One thing all this negativity did for me personally was to reaffirm my intention of not making the military a career, at least not within the enlisted ranks.

Boot camp—basic training—could have taken place somewhere on another planet for all I knew or cared. The only thing I remember about San Diego was that we were not going to see it up close until this training experience was nearly over. The weather was nice, and thousands of us were simply trying to survive and proceed on to the next step in fulfilling our military duty. I had heard that San Diego was a navy town. This was confirmed when my first liberty off base led me downtown into a sea of white hats—sailors—all appearing to have somewhere to go.

Like me, they were probably just happy to be back among the civilian population if only for a short time. This very large Naval Training Center where I was stationed had processed thousands of naval recruits since 1923. It closed down incrementally and ceased all military operations on April 30, 1997, as dictated by the federal Base Realignment and Closure Commission in 1993. Today it is listed on the National Register of Historic Places.

Thank God that I took marching band in high school, because that helped me get into the color guard ranks, which was a benefit later on in my boot camp experience. I learned how to stand in formation for two hours at four o'clock in the morning, moving forward a few feet every couple of minutes, until eventually our turn came to get our butts into the mess hall and quickly scarf down our morning chow. There is nothing quite like the smell of the morning chow, which was the same odor every morning, wafting over the grounds. It was not the smell I normally associated with breakfast, unless I was near the back alley of a bar. I also learned never to lie to my company chief petty officer, who was in charge of seeing to it that we made it through all the required boot camp segments before we could graduate.

One morning as we prepared for the daily personnel inspection out on the grinder—a huge cement area used for rank-and-file formations, marching drills, physical exercises, and inspections—I discovered that my undershirt was still damp from the previous day's hand laundering.

We were also required to have a certain number of these items folded in a specific manner and stored in our open-faced clothing locker at all times. They had to be stacked neatly inside the locker with a visible dress edge (perfectly folded and aligned), in addition to being dry. These lockers, along with our bunks, were thoroughly inspected each day while we were outdoors in company formation undergoing the morning personnel inspection. The potential problem could surface during this inspection when I had to display the inner liner in the neck of my T-shirt with my thumb so that the inspecting officer could check for any smudge or evidence of dirt on its inside threads. In my other hand I held my white navy hat inside out so that the officer could visually inspect the inside of it for cleanliness. The sweatband inside the hat had to be sparkling white, with not even a shadow of ground-in dirt. In the navy, cleanliness was plainly right up there next to godliness. Having a damp shirt would rub against my skin, possibly looking dirty or wet, which would be a "gig." Such a deficiency meant that one could be forced to squat down and "duck walk" around the company formation shouting "scrounge," which humiliated the hell out of the recruit being punished. I had made a promise to myself that this was not going to happen to me—ever.

A reservist in our company had noticed my predicament in the barracks that morning, and he volunteered to lend me one of his undershirts because he had extra ones from being in the reserves, as he told it. I panicked and took him up on his offer, then uneasily proceeded to the morning inspection along with everyone else. Standing in company formation with the white hat in one hand, turned inside out to expose the inner band, and the T-shirt thumbed inside out to show the neck line, we stood in formation, at the ready, for our daily routine. There happened to be another chief petty officer performing the inspection that morning, as sort of a guest inspector. Along with our company chief, he moved slowly down the line, one by one getting in our faces, occasionally commenting to our chief and sometimes to the individual recruit, about his readiness for inspection. As I recollect, he had reddish hair and kind of a ruddy complexion. He was pudgy and reminded me a little of the guy back home who sold me the boat. *Maybe this won't be so bad after all*, I thought.

It was much better if nothing was said, and my record to date had been very good. They came face to face with me, and the inspecting chief took one look at my shirt and said, "Is that your shirt, boy?" to which I answered, "Yes, sir." He asked me if I were in the reserves, to which I answered that I was not. Unknown to me, the reservist's shirts were slightly yellowed in comparison with our newly issued and very white ones. His next words were a bit unusual, but I complied. "Drop your trousers!" he ordered, and the second thing I had not thought about that morning was that our name was stenciled down at the bottom of the shirt in big black lettering along with our serial number. This is where any resemblance to the guy back home ended. I looked down and saw what looked like the devil laughing at me from a huge darkened hole in the ground.

Why me, Lord? went through my other half a brain, especially since I had never gotten away with a damned thing in school, or anywhere else for that matter, for practically my entire life. Why would my luck change now? "Is that your name, son?"

"No, sir," I replied, after which my company chief came up a little closer to me, and said in a slow, deliberate voice, "You're a fucking liar, aren't you?" to which I answered, "Yes, sir," for the second time that morning. There I stood, implicating my friend the reservist, making myself out to be a liar, and having no good excuse for what happened. I explained what had happened, but to no avail. At least I didn't get singled out in order to perform some physical punishment antics in front of my Company. Maybe they figured my situation was so pathetic that they felt sorry for me. I know my Company Chief was surprised that I was that stupid. Man, did I feel as stupid as a road-killed possum, but there wasn't a stinking thing I could do about it now. The earth was crumbling fast beneath my feet, and I was falling into an abyss of humiliation as we marched on to our next destination.

Later on that morning we took our company group pictures, and as we were getting positioned by the photographer for the camera shot, our chief yelled up at me while I was standing on the bleachers to not smile too much, because I wouldn't be smiling that afternoon. His remark grabbed my attention, and for the rest of the day I had that uneasy, half-sick feeling, similar to being called out by name and challenged to fight the school bully after school. I felt ashamed and very foolish all at the same time. All I really wanted now was to not have the reservist who loaned me his shirt be punished along with me. As it turned out he was not. Was it going to be as bad a punishment as when one of our recruits while sitting on a picnic table was ordered to lock his feet under its bench and do sit-ups with his arms and his rifle extended out over his head, until his back gave out? The answer was no, and I got off easy for reasons known only to the chief.

One of our assignments was to stand guard duty (fire watch) both inside and outside of the barracks during the night. While indoors we patrolled the floor of the barracks listening to the men snoring or talking in their sleep, and outside we guarded the clothes-drying lines with all the day's hand-scrubbed uniforms, underwear, socks, and hats. For my wrongdoings I pulled extra watch outside and got no sleep for a couple of nights, which was basically all of the punishment meted out, and the incident was never brought up again by anyone. No one in the unit said much of anything. I was never one seeking to attract a lot of attention, but I still felt bad, and as a result I worked even harder to prove that I was not a total screw-up. Hell, maybe I was learning something about teamwork and responsibility to others after all.

Diversity wasn't a word that was used much back in the early sixties. There were many races and a wide geographical spectrum of young men all trying to learn the same thing at the same time. In my high school we didn't have a lot of black students or many from the Philippines, and we darned sure didn't have slow-talking boys from Texas or Alabama walking the halls. There really wasn't time in boot camp to dwell on ethnic understanding, because we all were making the best out of a common set of circumstances and hoping to survive in order to reach the next level. We were forced to accept the situation, and if anyone had a problem with our collective makeup it would be theirs to own. This was not the place for initiating confrontation with anyone.

Later on in my enlistment as I worked and lived with everyone, I did have opportunities to form relationships and make some good friends with sailors and marines from a variety of ethnicities and backgrounds. Unfortunately, I also witnessed occasional prejudice and misunderstandings, but such problems were few and far between. The military took a dim view of any such issues; therefore, if racial intolerance and ignorance were a recruit's fixation, the consequences were severe. I never had any concerns or had to put aside my feelings toward anyone. In fact, I believe it may have been helpful to be from the Midwest since I didn't enter the military with many preconceived notions based upon bad experiences or deeply held prejudices. In addition, I had little knowledge of how segregated we were as a society even in the military, which was not that many years ago. My absence of problems along these lines was also a reflection of how I was reared and educated about how other people should be treated. It was not difficult.

During boot camp, all of us took a battery of written tests that were supposedly for the purpose of measuring our intelligence, aptitude, and anything else that the military chose to evaluate. I think they were taken to help determine which military occupation and specific training school would be the best fit for both the individual recruit and the navy. My score in the primary (a quasi-IQ) test was one of the highest in the company. All it meant at this point in time was that the test score and ten cents bought me a bottle of soda pop. I did notice that after the testing had been completed, the hard-assed company chief treated me a little better. I was also assigned to the color guard unit, which, as I indicated earlier, was a noticeable duty improvement and something of a status recognition thing. I took nothing for granted, but it did boost my confidence in my overall adaptation into military life and in myself a bit. I even garnered a wry grin out of the chief once in a while, but I think he was just a mean son of a bitch by nature. Screw him. Left, left, left-right-left . . . I'm outta here. Boot camp Graduation Day had arrived. We were sailors now, not just recruits any longer.

For my duty assignment after boot camp I had requested and received orders to the US Naval Hospital Corps School at San Diego, California. After I was granted a leave of two weeks at home, it was a return trip to San Diego for four months of training. The Greyhound Bus and I traveled back and forth from California to Nebraska three different times. It took forty hours to go one way, and cost about forty dollars round-trip, which was a good deal even back then. I saw a lot of country and met some interesting people during those trips, although I made it a point to keep to my own business.

Hospital corps school turned out to be a rewarding experience. The base was beautiful in its own right, with a substantial influence of Spanish architecture. For eight hours each day, Monday through Friday, we had classroom lectures, practical training exercises and validation testing over pharmacology, anatomy and physiology, first aid, and so on, administered by a highly professional staff of senior petty officer hospital corpsmen and commissioned officer nurses. Not only did they know the material from an academic perspective, but they related their medical experiences to us in detail. The classes were extremely well organized, accounting for every minute of the day, and the reinforcement mechanisms that were in place to help us retain this newly gained knowledge were excellent. After some of the initial classroom work, we were provided with opportunities to perform elemental medical duties at the large Balboa Naval Hospital located adjacent to the school. Here the nurses and more experienced corpsmen taught us the practical skills we would need to function as hospital corpsmen.

This duty assignment was almost like not actually being in the military. We still had to maintain our uniforms and keep our shoes shined for inspections, but compared to boot camp it was like being inspected by your own brother. The chief corpsmen in charge of our hospital corps school unit and the senior petty officers in charge of our classroom work were as close to civilians as one could expect in the military. I did well in this environment, and my attitude toward the area I chose to be involved in was entirely positive and met my expectations. I was soaking this stuff up.

The instructors and staff did a very good job of teaching us the criticality of the work involved and the medical discipline needed to do the job. There was classroom competition, participation, and an overall feeling of belonging to an identifiable entity whose mission was to do good for others. Additionally there was the benefit that we were learning something important. If those in hospital corps school made the wrong decision in choosing this as a military vocation, they were not allowed to continue on, and in fact they received counseling to find them a suitable military job skill. It was actually impressive to see firsthand the degree to which the navy cared about having the right personnel in the appropriate job.

As I alluded to earlier, San Diego was a mecca for sailors in those days. Everywhere I went there were sailors walking around town enjoying every minute they had away from their respective bases. In my case I spent a lot of my time exploring the downtown area where there were a sea of movie houses, tattoo parlors, and sidewalk barkers all trying to separate me from what little money I had. I don't know if I was ever around so many people yet felt as alone as I did then. I had friends in my class, but these were the same guys I was around twenty-four hours a day. It seemed that most of us wanted to get away from things when we had the chance to get off base. One of the main gathering points was the large YMCA, which had USO shows, and held regularly scheduled social activities such as dances. It was at least a place to go and relax for a while, since none of us were close to being of drinking age.

One night a classmate and I decided to get tattoos. We were on a mission. Back then, if you got a tattoo that became infected to the point where a visit to sick bay was required, a visit would also be made to your commanding officer. Getting tattoos was discouraged, but many if not most of us got them anyway. I got a small USN anchor on my left forearm, which could be used as the base for a large eagle perched on its top. Since I didn't know how much pain would be involved, and that a sparrow would look large on my spindly forearm, I spent the four bucks on the navy anchor tattoo only. It really didn't hurt much or take long to get. I kept it hidden from view and clean until it was healed out. It would not have looked good for a hospital corpsman to get an infection from a tattoo. Now I was officially a sailor, and believe it or not, I received a lot of compliments over the years on the small but conspicuous anchor. One place I did not receive a compliment from was from my dad the next time I was home. He had always said that none of his kids would ever come home with a damn tattoo. He'd probably observed some ridiculous-looking tattoos, in his opinion, and he didn't think it was a good idea to mark one's body permanently in that way.

I enjoyed my time at the Balboa Medical Complex, but all good things come to an end. It was time after four months to put in my request for where I wanted to be transferred after graduation from basic hospital corps school in March 1963. There were specialty schools such as X-ray or surgical technology, requiring much more training time, but I was more interested in seeing some of the world and getting to work, so I requested assignment to Hawaii. I had assumed that there must be a large naval hospital at Pearl Harbor, but I should have looked into this a bit more thoroughly. Our transfer orders arrived, and darned if I didn't get Hawaii—Oahu, in fact. *Lucky day for me*, was my initial reaction. However, one small problem lurked on the horizon. I had been assigned to the Fleet Marine Force and would not be going to Pearl Harbor. It turns out that the US Army, not the US Navy, had a large hospital on the island of Oahu. Not to worry, though, because the US Marine Corps had an air station on the other side of the island just waiting for me to join them for some fun and games. Why hadn't I heard more about this option during my schooling? I know they covered this Fleet Marine Force thing as a possibility, but alas, I evidently still had some bad listening skills from my high school days. Percentage-wise, the numbers of Fleet Marine Force corpsmen were not large in comparison to all of the other duty possibilities, so I didn't think it was something to be concerned about. I also thought that I had to volunteer for this type of duty assignment. Wrong on that one!

The marines do not have their own medical personnel but are supported in this respect by the US Navy. In fact, the Marine Corps is part of the Naval Department, but that is not something they wish to acknowledge or discuss. I did get Hawaii, though. It didn't make any difference now, since I would be going up the road just a short hop to the US Marine Corps' Camp Pendleton, located near Oceanside, California, for a five- to six-week stint to learn about the Marine Corps and how to wear the marine uniform, and to learn how to become a good field medical corpsman before being permanently assigned to a Marine Corps unit.

After I picked myself up from the floor, and without avenues for vigorous protest, I reluctantly buckled down to accepting the fact that I would not be wearing my navy blues or white uniforms for some time to come. I wasn't the only one from my training class to be assigned to the Fleet Marine Force, so at least I was in good company for what lay ahead. Some of these guys were not ecstatic with their assignments either. Trying to explain this to my family and relatives during my next leave home was a real challenge. "No, I am not a marine, but I will be with them for the next few years." Ouch! I remember my family remarking, "You didn't join the Marine Corps. How can they do this?" I just informed everyone that it would be all right, even though I didn't have a clue about what was about to happen. In truth, I had never wanted to be assigned to a ship anyway, so I talked myself into looking at this as a challenge, and after all, I was going to Hawaii. To be completely honest about it, I wasn't looking forward to working on a hospital ward either. It was a way to learn more and become more well-rounded, but the large hospital wards were not exactly where I wanted to be assigned for three more years. I just hoped I could pass muster from a physical conditioning perspective. Soaking wet, I weighed all of 165 pounds at six feet tall, so I was more or less an average, thin guy, in pretty good shape. In my mind, I pictured the marines all being six feet five inches tall and weighing in at two hundred pounds with a lot of muscle and mouth. It was also well known that marines and sailors didn't necessarily like each other very much. My new tattoo would go over well!

After another short leave home, it was off to Camp Pendleton. It was a good thing I made the visits back home when I could, because, unknown to me at the time, it would be a long time once I got to Hawaii before I made it back home again. At Camp Pendleton I found that the Marine Corps' expectations concerning hospital corpsmen were very modest regarding military prowess. Since the marines considered themselves to be the gold standard with respect to all things military, they would show us the way, or maybe it was really just their way. They were right. Naval medical personnel back then were not that much into the gung-ho military spirit of doing things. However, many of us could spit shine our shoes, march, and wear the uniform as well as, if not better than, some of them. I think our naval boot camp training was more demanding than they realized. During this training cycle we learned that we could improve in our endurance, strength, and all other physical conditioning attributes, which is what marines strive for. This training was a matter of pride to them, and we corpsmen had no desire to take anything away from that. We expected a certain degree of mutual respect, and we generally received it from them, even though they were hard to impress. The trick was in not trying to out-marine them but to focus on our own job responsibilities, which is why we were with them in the first place. They wanted no part of all this medical business, so all in all it was a clear and understood relationship.

During the next several weeks our medical training primarily focused on first-aid measures. We had to learn how to become field medical corpsmen as contrasted to corpsmen working in the direct hospital care environment, such as on a large ward. The proper medical treatments for heat exhaustion, heatstroke, shock, battlefield and accidental injuries, hemorrhage control, breathing problems, and a whole host of medical issues that may have to be dealt with in the field, possibly under battlefield conditions, were covered in detail. We were also lectured on the art of self-preservation under hostile conditions, so that we as corpsmen could be of maximum use to the highest number of patients. We were taught that the injured party was to be transported back to us for medical treatment in a secure area out of the line of fire. Even further, we were to use the patient as a shield if necessary to guard against ourselves being taken out of commission. This point was reinforced constantly during our training. There were not that many of us to go around, so we had to do our best to stay healthy. I didn't realize it then, but these directives would be difficult for me to comply with, except for the part about staying healthy. We practiced and simulated combat situations repeatedly, but nothing would nor could rise to the actual conditions and pressures, physical and emotional, that were involved in providing medical care under live-fire circumstances. I would later discover that my training at Camp Pendleton was invaluable in many ways, but many more actions and reactions resulted from the situation on the ground.

Camp Pendleton was also the place to learn how to adapt and acknowledge the Marine Corps way of doing things. The senior hospital corpsmen on staff trained us regarding all things medical, and the marine noncommissioned officers trained us on how to integrate within their units. We were in their house, and it was critical that we learn what was important to them and about their general culture. A significant part of this education was to fundamentally learn their expectations of us as we became a part of their operations. We participated in the arts of grenade throwing, firing a bazooka, and even operating a flame thrower. It was kind of neat to learn that I could pull the pin, but hold the release handle, even reinserting the pin to ensure that the grenade would not explode until I released the handle by throwing it away from me. The amount of devastation and power from such a small device was vastly underrated. One weapon that I liked but didn't get the chance to fire was the M-79 Grenade Launcher, which could accurately launch a grenade many times farther and higher than by throwing it manually. That may have been one of those things better left unlearned.

The weapon of choice or no choice for the field corpsmen was the .45-caliber semiautomatic pistol. It was heavy to handle and difficult to shoot well. In fact, the marines routinely joked with us that we could probably do more damage by throwing it at the enemy than by firing it at them. I would tend to agree with that assessment, at least in my case. We still had to qualify—pass a firing test—with it so that we could at least defend ourselves in close quarters should the need arise. The weapon did have extremely powerful knockdown ability, providing one of its rounds actually hit the target.

No one expected nor even wanted medical personnel to participate in supplying any firepower during a firefight. It wasn't that they didn't trust us, but the situation would have to be pretty dire if we were critical to the battle. We had our own job to do, and that was what we were expected to do. If the circumstance ever presented itself, I had no doubt that I could pull the trigger on whatever the target was who was trying to do me or my comrades harm. No corpsman I knew would have a problem firing on the enemy.

Overall, the Fleet Marine Force training was accomplished in a professional and organized manner, much as the basic hospital corps school was earlier. I graduated from the Field Medical Service School at Camp Pendleton, California, in May 1963. I have to admit that I didn't mind wearing the uniform of and acting a little like a marine. Maybe this was going to work out after all. At least I had a pocket in the trousers for my billfold, and going to the bathroom was not an unbuttoning marathon as with navy bell-bottoms.

FOUR

Aloha

It was time to leave Oceanside, California, and move on to the island of Oahu, Hawaii—to Kaneohe Marine Corps Air Station, which was located on the far and less populated windward side of the island from Pearl Harbor, Honolulu, and Waikiki Beach. Originally a Naval Air Station, the base was attacked shortly before the hit at Pearl Harbor on December 7, 1941. Multiple strafing runs over the air station destroyed nearly all the planes on the ground and killed eighteen sailors and two civilians in addition to wounding sixty-nine others. The base was commissioned as a marine base in 1952 after the navy had moved operations to Barbers Point Naval Air Station. It was a well-laid-out facility on a very scenic part of Oahu, and my first impression was that I wanted to see much more of the area at my first opportunity.

I was assigned to a battalion medical aid station that furnished medical support to one of the infantry marine battalions (Second Battalion, Fourth Marines, First Marine Brigade [FMF]) stationed on the base. Our battalion consisted of four infantry companies in addition to weapons, engineering, and other headquarters and service personnel, of which the medical group was a part. The infantry companies were named E (Echo), F (Fox), G (Golf), and H (Hotel). At the aid station were a doctor and approximately forty hospital corpsmen who conducted the daily sick call in addition to treating the walk-in patients, providing immunizations,

4.1 Image of battalion insignia. Our battalion commander, Lieutenant Colonel Joseph R. "Bull" Fisher, added the phrase "The Magnificent Bastards" in 1964 to the Second Battalion, Fourth Marines insignia. Photo of insignia courtesy of H. Krentel, fellow hospital corpsman

and being responsible for everyone's medical records. Many of us were assigned to the individual marine infantry companies as their designated medical corpsmen. A marine company consisted of approximately 125 to 140 personnel distributed over three platoons and a headquarters group comprising the company commander, first sergeant, gunnery sergeant, staff sergeant, radioman, and other personnel as assigned.

Manpower permitting, two hospital corpsmen were assigned to each platoon, along with a senior company medical corpsman as part of the company headquarters group. For reporting purposes, the platoon medical corpsmen reported to the senior company corpsman, who in turn reported to the battalion aid station chief petty officer. I began my experience as a platoon hospital corpsman but became the senior corpsman of the company when I was promoted to petty officer third class, which is an E-4 noncommissioned officer rank and equal to a corporal in the Marine Corps. I was assigned to Company E—Echo Company—from near the beginning until the end of my time with the Marine Corps.

The marines spent much of their time in physical conditioning, weapons training, classroom participation, and conducting routine preparedness drills. If they carried out an operation of any duration, we accompanied them. If they left the barracks for a five-mile run, we ran, too. If one- or two-day military exercise was conducted out in the field, we corpsmen also took part in it. The company corpsman conducted company sick call each day, and if necessary, further treatment could be obtained at the battalion aid station that was located close to the marine barracks, where my platoon corpsmen and I were quartered.

Over time, we corpsmen and our respective marine units became closely interwoven. There was always some good-natured bantering asserting that corpsmen were not marines and so on, which led to the occasional back-and-forth about the best military branch. When you are in a minority of thirty to two, some of this behavior would be expected. This was a unique situation where we needed each other, and there was no tolerance from the higher ranks for any serious interservice disrespect. We were all part of the same unit, and we had to pull together in order to fulfill our assigned mission. If things were ever to get drastic, we could always play the card of, "Do you know who keeps the records of your shots?" The implied threat was that they would have to get their shots all over again if their records were lost. Some of the guys were leery of getting inoculations, so we didn't joke around about it. And also, if any tampering with medical records ever took place, a court-martial hearing would result.

I personally took a lot of pride in how I wore my uniform, whether it was navy blues or the marine kakis. The vast majority of the time we wore the marine uniform, but we were not issued their dress blues, which were reserved for the most formal Marine Corps functions, were highly symbolic, and only a marine could wear them. No other military personnel I was aware of were allowed to have two nearly complete sets of uniforms from different service branches. There were basically three types of marine uniforms we as corpsmen were expected to wear. The utilities (green field uniform with bloused trouser bottoms and matching cap), cotton khakis for everyday work use, and the dress khaki that had to be dry-cleaned. I had my uniforms starched, pressed, or whatever the situation called for, including the appropriate headwear. I made it a point to always present a sharp appearance, for I was not going to have any marine think that I was not as capable of wearing the uniform as well as he could.

Everyone knew their respective roles, even considering that most of us were just eighteen or nineteen years old. If any lessons in exhibiting maturity were needed, plenty of sergeants and chiefs were around to set things straight. The next two years were about as good from a duty standpoint as one might expect being in the military. Not only was Hawaii a beautiful place, but I got along well with the marines as well as my fellow corpsmen. A final comment concerning uniforms brings up a humorous anecdote. On the nonutility uniforms, marines have their stripes indicating their military rank sewn onto the upper sleeves of both arms. Commissioned officers, however, have nothing on their sleeves, only their metal bars or other insignia prominently fastened to their shirt collars. Hospital corpsmen have their insignia shown only on the upper left sleeve. Enlisted personnel meeting an officer while walking around the base were required to salute, and the officer then returned the salute. On more than one occasion, marines coming toward me from my right side would salute me, thinking I was some young lieutenant, especially since many of them were towheads, too. Once they realized that I was not an officer, they would say, "Dog-gone you, Doc." Then we would both have a good laugh at no great expense to either party.

Hawaii was gorgeous, even if the locals didn't exactly toss leis around our necks on a routine basis. We didn't have the tourist money to throw around, and possibly our manners were not so refined at times, especially on Friday and Saturday nights. In other words, we sort of asked to be treated as second-rate some of the time. Even though the local economy was stimulated in large part because of the money we spent in the area, some residents appeared to have an attitude of merely tolerating our presence. Even with some of our faults, their attitude came across a bit too strong at times. The welcome-to-Hawaii smiles were largely saved for the tourists.

Unless I had to work at the battalion aid station on the weekends, I normally slept in on Saturday mornings. After getting dressed in my civvies (civilian clothes) and making a quick trip to the mess hall, I caught a suicide cab to Honolulu or Waikiki for the day. A suicide cab was an older-model automobile with so-called suicide doors, but I always thought that they had this nickname because the drivers drove at a fairly rapid clip up, over, and through the mountains via the Pali Highway. (The term "suicide doors" refers to a four-door car where both the front and back door handles are close to the center of the car.) Additionally, I couldn't always be positive that these drivers were fully awake and alert. I enjoyed going to the afternoon movies with my popcorn, candy, and large-sized soda pop well in hand. I liked movies of any type, and this small break in the daily military base routine of working, eating, and sleeping served as an escape for me, even if I didn't realize it at the time.

After the movie I normally took a bus to Waikiki, where all the tourists and the upscale hotels and shops were. Honolulu was not the place to hang out later at night, especially if traveling alone. One of my favorite places to eat in Waikiki was a restaurant with a large charcoal pit located near the center of the main dining room. I'd select one of their uncooked steaks, take it over to the grate, and grill my own dinner. The steak accompanied by a potato, tossed salad, and baked beans was a good deal economically, especially when I didn't burn my steak. Since I wasn't old enough to go into the bars, I walked around Waikiki taking in the sights and occasionally watching the sunset down by the beach. A lot of airline stewardesses and schoolteachers visited Waikiki during the summer months, which was great for girl watching, but most of them weren't looking for young military guys with little money and even less hair. Admittedly, I was not an old hand at meeting women either. Later that night I would book a return cab back to the base, stop by the aid station to shoot the bull with whoever was on duty, then hit the rack. Sundays were spent washing clothes, shining shoes, writing letters, and otherwise preparing for the week ahead. There was a club on base, referred to as the "E Club," for the enlisted personnel to have a beer or three. I went there a few times, but between the military police and some of the patrons getting out of control, I didn't make it a habit. Beer, loud music, a crowded environment with buzzed eighteen- to twenty-year-old guys, in addition to all the alcohol-enriched machismo made for a raucous, Wild West atmosphere. I don't remember any women being there either.

During my two years on Oahu we performed military exercises over all types of terrain, including amphibious training, in nearly all weather conditions. We made a couple of excursions over to the big island of Hawaii, where we walked over miles of volcanic rock in the higher elevations. On the island of Molokai we walked through fields of pineapples, which meant no one went to bed hungry. We wonder why our public relations concerning the civilians suffered from time to time. I don't think they liked their pineapples being tossed or kicked around like footballs. Of course the few marines who purposely damaged the fields spent a few hours doing extra duty in addition to cleaning up any mess they made as a result of their immaturity. If a farmer complained to our commanding officer, there would be hell to pay for each one of us, including our officers in charge.

If we had absolutely nothing else to do or nowhere else to go, we always found time to run a few miles every week. A large hill on the base resembled a small version of the Devils Tower rock formation in Wyoming. The marines in charge liked nothing better than to jog to this hill, run up it as far as they could, then turn back around and run back to the barracks. I don't remember how far all of this was, but I could count every time on at least one or two heat exhaustion cases on the way back. We were not wearing running shorts and tennis shoes but were in uniform with pack, weapons, helmets, and boots. My side hurt so much on some of these trips that I almost fell out of formation. Even though I was bringing up the rear, something about seeing the guy up ahead of me working his ass off spurred me on to not quit.

If practice makes perfect, our company should have been a war machine from a physical conditioning perspective, because during these two years I believe that I walked and ran more than I had in my entire life to date. Being in excellent physical shape was of key importance and certainly would be in a duty station not so far in the future. The day President Kennedy was assassinated in 1963 we were "attacking" a mock-up village (shades of Vietnam possibly) during an exercise when the message of this tragedy was received. Operations immediately ceased, and we headed for the barracks, no one saying hardly a word on the long walk back. Thoughts of the assassination of Abraham Lincoln went through my mind, and it got a little scary to realize how primitive we still were for being supposedly such a highly civilized nation.

I had long been a supporter of President Kennedy. In high school we had a mock election and chose Kennedy over Nixon. I admired how he did his job, and I thought he had a great deal of charisma. He was appealing to the younger citizens, and as the age of the populace increased, so did the support for Nixon. It was a generational thing in part, but there was also substantial support for JFK's brothers. Not everyone that day was taken aback, but I'm not sure any of us wanted to think about President Lyndon Johnson (LBJ) being our commander in chief. Justified or not, LBJ didn't appear to have the straight-and-narrow image that Kennedy did. I remember thinking of him a bit like the Foghorn Leghorn rooster character in the Looney Tunes cartoons.

The marines did the best they could to duplicate actual combat situations. These operations would range from large-scale, battalion-size tactical situations involving ships, tanks, and landing craft attacks on the beach to lesser manpower maneuvers such as the mock village firefights mentioned earlier. Even though only a medical corpsman, I sensed that the larger and more complex the exercise was, the more confusing and chaotic it appeared to be militarily.

These war games included having attacks on the "enemy" forces along with the firing of hundreds of blank, but nonetheless loud, rounds. There were designated casualties for the corpsmen to treat and disposition, including medical evacuation procedures. The simulated injuries were not without imagination, as I remember seeing everything from a sucking chest wound to severe head trauma. This training was good for us, as we had to learn to use the medical dressings and equipment just as if they were real-life circumstances so that we did it right. Putting on a compress dressing to stop the bleeding doesn't do any good if it isn't applied correctly. While there was no way to perfectly mimic battlefield conditions, the exercises definitely gave us an idea of what to expect. They even added in the patients yelling and on-the-spot reviews by senior experienced corpsmen concerning errors made and overall job performance. We did these drills repeatedly, which was a good thing, because when these skills were needed, it would be too late to have to think it all through first. Our reactions had to be instinctual. We did have at least one exercise where live fire was scattered overhead as we crawled through an obstacle course toward the objective we were to overtake. I am confident that had I stood up, I wouldn't have had to worry about going to South Vietnam.

Located on our base was a large naval medical dispensary that provided medical services for all base military personnel and their dependents. It was basically our base hospital as well as a referral point for anyone needing a level of medical care they could not get at the battalion aid station. We field hospital corpsmen were given an opportunity to be temporarily assigned to the dispensary for a period of six months. Here we received more in-depth medical training and had the opportunity to work in a more advanced medical setting. At the dispensary, I learned how to suture lacerations—but only on marines, not their dependents—performed some elemental laboratory testing, such as analyzing urine and blood slides; drew blood samples; gave inoculations to military and civilian personnel; and assisted in X-ray and surgery activities.

We normally had a supervisor nearby in case questions arose relative to performing our duties. Sometimes, however, the supervisor was not present, and I would be on my own. Usually that was not a problem, and I would work through any small issue in an efficient and correct manner. A physician on duty once asked me to draw a blood sample from an infant. I acknowledged his order and proceeded to look for a suitable vein from which to obtain the sample. This was my youngest patient involving such a request, and I was unable to locate a vein from which to draw the sample. I was basically in over my head. The tiny patient was in his mother's arms and was not happy about even being in this environment. I went back to the doctor and told him of my problem, and he said to draw it from his neck area, to which I responded that I could not perform that procedure. He said, "Okay then," and he abruptly went with me to the mother and infant along with a nurse who happened to be in the area. He told the nurse and me to hold the baby securely with his head slightly down toward the floor, and to remain as steady as possible. The whole thing looked odd and unlike anything I'd ever seen. He then efficiently and quickly drew the blood sample. I thought to myself, *This is why you are the doctor, and I am the corpsman.* I also knew that I made the only correct decision for me. The nurse agreed and said she wouldn't have done it either, which helped with my confidence going forward. Medical officer or not, I learned that no amount of pressure was going to make me do something medically stupid for the patient or myself.

I especially liked working in the surgical operating room, which was also the dispensary emergency room, more than in any of the other areas within the facility. It was intriguing to observe the cases and assist the surgeons in practicing their skills. As mentioned earlier, corpsmen were not allowed to perform some medical procedures on the dependents, although we were allowed to inject the local anesthetic lidocaine near an area to be sutured so that it would be a painless ordeal. Sometimes, on the smaller lacerations, the trauma associated with this injection, especially with small children, was almost as bad as the suturing would have been. I was always glad in these cases when the doctor could do just as well by applying butterfly bandages to close the wound. Overall, I felt that I was performing work that seemed more intellectually stimulating and challenging. I also liked walking around in the green surgical scrubs and feeling good about helping people. It also gave my self-confidence a boost from a job performance perspective. I had made up my mind even before these experiences that if I were to ever become a medical doctor, I would be a surgeon. It never hurts to dream a little.

One of my last training segments during my rotation at the dispensary was assisting with the large daily clinical sick calls for the military dependents, when the mothers and their children came in for a wide range of medical issues. This was my least favorite part of the overall training scheme. Working in the clinic was a good experience for me, but one aspect I particularly disliked was when small infants needed injections. In those days the doctors prescribed penicillin for any type of upper respiratory problem or suspected infections or almost anything else, so it appeared. The problem was that it had to be administered with a large-bore needle into the child's buttock. Imagine trying to inject something resembling white liquid glue into a baby's butt. It was not a free-flowing liquid, and the whole experience normally bordered on being traumatic, especially for the little guy. Not that there was anything wrong with the procedure; it just was not for me day in and day out. The needle looked as big as the baby's butt, which to me didn't seem right. I had to face the fact that maybe there was no problem, other than my problem hearing and seeing the babies in such pain. No one else in the room where the shots were given liked it either. I therefore had to accept that and move on, at least until the day would come when I would be smart enough to improve the procedure.

The experience of working at the dispensary helped round out my medical training and once again reflected the thoroughness built into the military's approach to blending education with on-the-job training. Some of the more senior hospital corpsmen were very adept at their jobs from both an academic and practical perspective. I admired their depth of knowledge and job skills. Some of these guys were on their second enlistment, so they already had four to five years or more of experience. Where I was headed, there would be some other traits and attributes that I would need, but I just didn't know it yet. After completing the six months of temporary assignment, it was back to my marine buddies at the battalion—back to the real world and my daily work routine.

During the evening hours most of us hung around the battalion aid station, not only to bother the corpsmen on duty, but to shoot the bull about anything and everything. The aid station resembled a college fraternity of sorts, where we could spend some time together as a group. Sometimes a young marine would sheepishly stick his head in the door and ask, "You guys have time to look at me?" The answer was always, "Yes, of course we do, get on in here." We knew why we were there. Some of us counted days and marked them off the calendar while others just kept a running total in their heads of the days left until their release from active duty. I met few bona fide volunteers (guys who actually wanted to join the military) and even fewer who were going to reenlist, but things do change over the course of four years. Who knows?

More than once, some of the senior career corpsmen spoke with me about Officer Candidate School (OCS). There were some, but not many, opportunities to become a commissioned officer without possessing a college degree. One way was to be recommended by one's supervisory personnel to undergo an evaluation concerning Officer Candidate School requirements. I did think about it seriously, but it would have involved a longer time commitment than I was willing to make, even if I were to receive a commission. I would also not be a hospital corpsman any longer. I did not pursue it further, but it did feel good to at least be considered for such a possibility. Having been promoted more quickly than some others in my medical unit, I would actually become kind of a salty dog (an older and more experienced sailor is thought to be salty from all his time at sea)—a third-class petty officer by the time the active-duty part of my enlistment was over. Even so, I was far from being highly experienced.

I don't recall any lengthy discussions about South Vietnam. We had been told about the military advisers assisting in that part of the world, but there was no real connection with us, just rumors that we would be eventually heading over there if the US role became more than advisory in nature. Many of us actually believed that the United States would not commit large masses of ground troops. Korea was not that far in the past, and I personally believed that we as a country were not anxious to go to war. In addition, as far as any of us knew, there were no combat military units in Vietnam at this time. We would be among the first major detachments to go. In my case, I don't think that I wanted to face up to going, but I did want those in power to settle it from a decision-making aspect.

Eventually as the news accounts became more and more about Vietnam it seemed inevitable that something was going to change regarding our foreign policy. One of the reasons that our involvement wasn't discussed much out in the open on my level was because of the uncertainty of when it would happen and of course how things would go down. After all, we occasionally heard within the enlisted ranks, "Ours is not to reason why, ours is but to do or die."

Very early in the spring of 1965, word came that we would be moving out from Hawaii. Finally they were filling in some of the blanks! There wasn't time to tell anyone what was going on, and we definitely weren't allowed to discuss anything with anyone about troop movements anyway, even if they had told us where we were headed. Then one evening, with no warning, we immediately packed up all of our possessions and boarded buses for transport to a waterfront I had never been to during all of the time I was stationed on Oahu. I had just taken a leave at Christmas, which was a good thing, since it would now be a while before I would be returning home. We had an idea where we were headed, but no one told us a thing.

FIVE

Okinawa-Bound

Waiting for us was a very large ship with a funny sounding name, the *Peter Rabbit.* Actually, I think this was a nickname for the USS *Paul Revere* APA-248. It felt as if I were in an old World War II movie as we made our way onto our new ride and what soon would be our new living quarters. I imagined for a second that I spotted Jimmy Stewart, or maybe more appropriately John Wayne, somewhere in the crowd, but no, this wasn't a movie. It was really just us leaving for an unspecified destination, for an uncertain length of time. One thing was fairly certain: this was not going to be some weeklong maneuver or brief military exercise, because we left nothing back at the base.

The marines, including myself, were like fish out of water on the large ship. We were not on a boat, but a ship, we were reminded. We weren't informed about our destination, how long we would be at sea, or any details of real significance. The main concern nagging at my gut was that my family would not know what was going on, meaning they wouldn't know exactly where I was. This would cause them stress, especially my mother, which really pissed me off. I regularly wrote home, and my family wrote even more frequently than I did. It seemed there was always something going on at home, and I looked forward to hearing all the latest local news. There was absolutely nothing I could do about this situation but wait it out. I was not alone in this regard. There was no doubt about it; this was no drill. I knew my family would figure it out once my letters didn't come, or they may read or hear about our exploits once the media got wind of them.

There was an air of seriousness unlike anything I had been a part of during previous military exercises in Hawaii. Maybe it was because I didn't hear the normal bitching about things. The marines were in charge, and I was along for the ride, to wherever it was and however long it would take to get there. No more security blanket of the aid station as my little fraternity house to count on. There was now a sense of every man for himself, or was that just my imagination working a little overtime? Possibly I was simply feeling a bit isolated, because from now on I would stay with my marine company day in and day out organizationally. The battalion aid station would be staffed by those who were not assigned to individual marine units. Overall an uneasy and melancholy mood was evident as we stood out on the deck of the ship and waved "So long" to Hawaii. I plainly had the feeling that I would not be passing this way again anytime soon.

We hit the high seas stacked like sardines from top to bottom in our new quarters, but it was not bad, considering how many of us were bunking in the ship's belly. The movement of our vessel through the ocean waves made for good sleeping conditions, at least for me. The food on board was darned good, and we had plenty of time to roam all around the deck observing what was going on and watching the sailors going about their work. In short order, many of the guys became seasick, but I was fortunate enough not to have such issues. I didn't have a secret stash of seasickness pills or anything, but I retrieved whatever was available from sick bay for those needing them. Maybe it was all those carnival rides at the county fairs back in Kansas that preconditioned me. Who knows? We corpsmen helped out with sick call in the medical facilities on board, but that still provided us with time to become more than a little bored. I wandered up to the deck at night to watch our ship plow through the waves as if they weren't there. In rough seas, the water splashed over the bow and onto the deck, and I could feel and see the ship rise up high on the waves, then splash down quickly over and over in perfect rhythm with their motion. For a landlubber like myself, I never tired of it. When the water was smooth I ventured forward to the front of the bow and just gazed out in front of the ship in all directions as it sliced through the ocean below without the slightest waver.

The entire dynamic of being on this ship was something that I wanted to absorb, because I didn't know if I would have another chance. I had never been out on the ocean so far from good old terra firma; therefore, it was comforting to occasionally see lights from other vessels far off in the distance. I didn't feel quite so isolated knowing that others were out here, too. The sailors were used to it, although I believe that some of them also enjoyed peering out over the ocean in the quiet of night. The reflection from the moon on the water as it followed along with us on our trek was remarkable. It was a beautiful sight, and at that point I realized that I liked nearly everything about the ocean. The smell of the salt water in the air, the sound of our ship passing through the water, accompanied at times by the noisy seabirds flirting with the whitecaps tipping the waves—all these things I felt fortunate to witness, even if briefly. After seeing how hard some of the sailors worked, I hadn't changed my mind about not wanting shipboard duty, but I could grow to love being on the sea.

It took us approximately three weeks to reach the island of Okinawa. I don't recall precisely when they informed us of our destination, but it was later during our voyage. Any communication was largely by word of mouth, so everyone kept their antennae perked up at all times. Unfortunately, with this form of communication, rumors were often rampant. We knew that Vietnam was a destination at some future point, we just didn't know when nor how it would play out. A few guys wanted to go directly over there and get it over with, but most of us were glad to see Okinawa, if only for the short time we would take up residence there. Few of us knew much about the historical significance of Okinawa relative to our country, only that there were intense battles on these islands during World War II for which we paid a heavy price.

I was relieved that we would now be able to send and receive mail. The day we arrived in Okinawa we made the trip to the base—Camp Hansen—in a long convoy of troop transport trucks originating from where we had docked. It was cloudy and damp, but many people standing along the roadways were waving and smiling at us as we passed by. The island was picturesque but appeared extremely poor in terms of housing and transportation. After almost two years in Hawaii, I was anxious to visit somewhere different, even if it meant we would pay a price for it in the future. The military base was huge, very clean, and a welcome sight for us ol' sea pirates. The military employed a large number of local civilian personnel to work in the base stores and laundry in addition to performing other functions on the base as necessary. My uniforms were never so well pressed nor smelled as clean as when we were stationed in Okinawa.

Nearly every day it was up and out to the street for a little morning jog of a few miles—"Left, left, yur left . . . right . . . left," singing and chanting some silly, sometimes obscene little ditty to go along with our cadence. It helped pass the time, and the psychologists would likely say this helped shape and bond us as a unit. We were getting back in good physical shape and building up our endurance from sitting around on the ship for three weeks. We didn't go on any major military exercises such as those in Hawaii, just run, run, and run. I think we were conditioning and merely marking time until we were ordered to move out. Supposedly, all of us were ready to go. I think everybody realized where we were headed next, and it definitely was not a return trip to Hawaii.

We were granted liberty off base almost every evening and weekend. The exceptionally clean and very well-kept base was in stark contrast to the surrounding area, which comprised bars and shanties along with a host of other ways to separate us from our money. Scores of working girls were waiting right outside the base gates in hopes of discovering marines and other military personnel ready to become better acquainted. Bars stretched along the main highway as far as the eye could see, including in the smaller towns a few miles down the road from the base. The jukeboxes played all the American songs one could ever want to hear, and if I wanted some company to sit by me, all I had to do was buy both of us some drinks. Some of the young women were very attractive, and it was a good time just to relax, drink a few beers, listen to "My Girl" on the jukebox, and maybe dance a little. Basically it was a chance to spend time with someone not in the military. As long as a guy bought drinks and didn't act like a cheapskate, one of the girls would keep him company until the bar closed if that's what he wanted.

It was prudent to remember that we were guests in Okinawa, and not to act like ill-mannered, drunken bums. From what little bad behavior I saw, the military police didn't accept many excuses, and they would directly escort you to confinement. I didn't barhop that much, but I found a small establishment where I was comfortable spending time. Besides, one employee at this bar was particularly nice, friendly, and otherwise good company. For a price, I could make financial arrangements with the mama-son in charge of the bar to take things even further with some, but not all, of the girls, if that was my aim. I was not interested in the ones who went with the guys for a short-time (thirty-minute) encounter, as some of them so frequently offered for an agreed-upon charge. There was another price to pay for having too much fun, though. Contracting a venereal disease was a very plausible risk, most notably in the form of gonorrhea, and the Marine Corps took a dim view of their people being diagnosed with such medical problems—so dim, in fact, that any marine contracting a venereal disease would have the privilege of having his name posted in the mess hall for all to see when they went there to eat.

I didn't agree with this tactic, and I know our doctors didn't either, but it was the commanding officer's policy. To my way of thinking, it just led to more guys hiding their ailments. As a preventive measure, there were random surprise inspections (referred to as "pecker checks") performed by the on-duty hospital corpsmen. These examinations were held in the early morning hours, in the barracks, before anyone had a chance to take their morning pee. Anyone having a visible problem, such as a sore or an infectious discharge, had a laboratory slide prepared by the corpsman for later microscopic examination and a follow-up with a medical officer. By performing these examinations, anyone having an issue could receive the proper treatment before further damage was done to them or others with whom they may have sexual relations. Overall, there were not large numbers of problems for all the sexual activity supposedly going on, but there were enough cases to warrant the effort. Pecker checks were not my favorite duty as a medical corpsman. Even though I understood why they were necessary, I was more than happy to let someone else do them. I would rather give the many inoculations that we would all have to receive before leaving for South Vietnam.

We were only stationed in Okinawa for five or six weeks, but during that time I had the chance to experience at least a brief but enjoyable glimpse of Asian culture. I had always found Asian people to be extremely polite and friendly from my days in Hawaii, and the good people of Okinawa only supported these impressions. It was probably a good thing that we weren't in Okinawa longer, because I was spending too much time with my little friend in the bar that I frequented. One night we did venture to her apartment away from the bar, which was a step in the right direction as far as I was concerned. We were just getting comfortable, having a couple of drinks and making small talk, when all at once she looked at my watch. She quickly topped off the liquor bottle with water and said that I would have to leave. Not knowing what was going on, I did just that, and as we were saying good-bye in her doorway I noticed a large, older, marine sergeant type getting out of a cab and walking our way. I said good evening and hastily got into the cab. As I looked back I saw a confused look on his face, and I think she was smiling and waving at me. He was obviously her "keeper," which is someone who helps with her rent and other expenses as part of their relationship. I still liked her anyway, but I was not to see her again, and I didn't need to worry about venereal disease.

The word was passed down that we soon would be boarding another ship. It appeared that this was what we had been waiting for. This trip wouldn't be nearly as long as the one from Hawaii to Okinawa. Even though we were all old hands at this sailing stuff now, the whole thing still felt surreal to me and probably a lot of the other guys, too. We were drawing near to the point of no return concerning South Vietnam. For the first time in a long time, I had a fleeting resentment in being attached to the Marine Corps. After all, I didn't sign up to be in the marines, and I was not a marine. Not knowing the what, when, and where of things was not helpful either. Then, after reality set in, I realized that we would all be in the same boat, in the most literal sense. Maybe I was a little scared. So long, Okinawa. It was fun while it lasted. Maybe I'd see you on the flip side.

SIX

Hitting the Beach: Hello, South Vietnam

After a day or two on board the ship (I don't remember the name), we were given a short briefing, officially informing us that we were under orders to be among the first contingent of combat forces (not advisers) that would soon be landing in South Vietnam. They told us that the South Vietnamese government had requested our help, and that we would be fighting alongside their military against the North Vietnamese communists and the Viet Cong insurgent forces. We were informed that the US government had determined that we would execute this action in the name of our country. From an overall perspective we were going there to stem the advance of communism in that area of the world. I can't say that this information took anyone by surprise. It was good to hear the official reason for our involvement, but it didn't help lessen the angst about what soon would be occurring. I didn't question the reason for what we were doing or the chance of success at that time, but neither did any of us want to be sitting off the coast of South Vietnam waiting to lay it all on the line. I knew very little about the history of this country we were about to inhabit, and even less about the history of our commitments to their people.

I believe that the United States had honorable motives concerning our presence in that part of the world, but no one spoke about how long we would be there. How could they? I'm sure that every man and woman about to be involved in something this historic wanted that question answered. There was no official tour of duty yet established, and except for the experienced career personnel I doubt anyone was thinking that far into the future.

As we approached the coast of South Vietnam we were supplied with live ammunition. That abruptly put the reality of the situation in proper focus. I loaded the magazine(s) of my .45-caliber pistol and took note of the fact that hardly a foot above my bed was a baby-faced marine lying in his rack with live grenades attached to his gear. There was a lot of chatter, and last-minute preparations had begun for our landing the next day. I made sure my medical bag was stocked with all the battle dressings (large rectangular padded dressing with cloth straps for securing tightly to the patient), gauze, tape, scissors, morphine syringes, tourniquet, medicinal supplies, and other essentials that I could fit in it. It was so fat that I could barely zip the pouches shut. Even though I knew from past experience, I still reviewed over and over in my mind where everything was located in my bag so that I could quickly retrieve specific items I might need. I couldn't afford to be fumbling around in my medical bag in the dark of night or when someone was in distress. (Truth be told, I was still all thumbs when I came upon my first casualty in the field. I had to look in my bag for almost everything I needed.) The last evening on board ship was fairly normal, but low key. We ate a good meal, showered, and no doubt said a few prayers as we tried to get some sleep, waiting for morning to come. I have to give the noncommissioned officers credit, for they made the rounds to all of their men, checking and rechecking with them that they were prepared for tomorrow. I doubt that many of us slept real soundly that night.

After chow and getting ready for battle as much as humanly possible, we all assembled near the ship's outer rail the next morning. It was a beautiful spring day in early May 1965. Row by row of five or so men, we organized ourselves for crawling down the large amphibious net draped like a big twine spiderweb over the side of the ship, and extending down into the much smaller transport boat below. I remember the swells being so large that the net would stretch out and then constrict in sync with the waves. At the same time, the smaller boat we were loading into was constantly positioning itself so as not to bang up against the mother ship, yet staying in close enough to allow us to control the tautness of the nets. If I were to somehow fall to the water between the watercraft they would almost certainly crush me, but if I were lucky, I could simply fall into the floor of the boat that we were crawling down into and only break a few body parts.

Was I more afraid of what we were now about to do, or what we would be getting into later this morning? I was trying my best not to show by my facial expressions the wide range of emotions that were overrunning my thought process. I had to get a grip on myself and give attention to the immediate challenge at hand, which was to safely get my ass down into the landing craft. As much as possible, I needed to mitigate my fears and anxiety so that I could function and do my job when the time came. It didn't pay to look too far ahead.

I'm sure I wasn't the only one whose legs were a little wobbly when the sergeant gave the command for our specific group to move out. I had already said my last-minute prayers. *Here we go*, I thought to myself, as I crawled up and over the side of the ship onto the net, grabbing it like I had never grabbed anything in my life, making sure my boots were squarely placed on the net rungs, and trying not to let my body pull me too far back, relying on my arm and leg strength to keep me hugging the web. It was a long ways down. I'd forgotten how heavy the weight of the gear and my own body was as their combined mass tugged at my arms. Gravity was also working against me, pulling me down into the boat. I knew I should have worked on those pull-ups more. I made it a point to concentrate on my every movement as I repositioned my hands and feet one more step down the net, ever closer to the landing craft. Never did I claim to be the most coordinated person in the world, but I had no intention of falling off this damned thing because I was not paying close enough attention to my surroundings. Had I been curious enough to look down at the water, even though we were not supposed to, I would have seen the waves churning and splashing against both of the vessels. It certainly would have been much better if the water were calm and not buoying the small boat up and down. One poor guy had his foot slip through the net, leaving him hanging almost upside down, but he righted himself and proceeded on down into the boat. I was relieved for him and for me, because none of his grenades fell off his gear.

We had no real clue of what lay ahead for us. Was it going to be as bad as some of those World War II movies portrayed as we landed on the beach? We went through the motions much in the same manner as we had during our practice drills in similar exercises back in Hawaii. After we had made our way down into the small navy boats, they piloted them in what felt like circular patterns, positioning us in the correct formation for landing on the beach. I don't remember feeling that scared, but I may have been beyond scared and into the terrified zone. I wasn't sure of the others, but I personally wanted to get it over with one way or the other. I think we all probably felt the same way. We couldn't actually see over the side of the boat since we were hunkered down in its bottom. After a warning shout, down went the front of the landing vessel. Someone yelled, "Go, go, go!" over and over again, and we ran off our boat, sinking immediately up to our private parts in the warm waters of the South China Sea. We advanced and spread out laterally, as we ran forward onto the beach heading for a tree line as fast as our legs would move. We met no organized resistance at this stage of our landing, and we proceeded to dig in, excavating foxholes into the sand with our small field shovels. We stayed there until the time came to move inland for the night. I think this was one of the few times I had ever dug a foxhole. At this point in time it didn't matter from a psychological perspective if we met resistance or not. Since we had no idea of the magnitude of the perils ahead, we were prepared and geared up for whatever form they would take.

I don't recall that anyone ever complained about not getting shot at or not being in a firefight that day, but I do remember that all of us were on constant high alert in case things changed. We were wired, and emotions were running high as we formed our initial impressions of South Vietnam. Its stark beauty and lack of any evident civilization except for the few people who were standing by the beachfront is what I remember at first glance. They appeared friendly, and I think they wore colorful attire. Maybe they were glad to see us. I was glad to see them. Their being in plain sight kind of took the edge off our angst in a small way, at least in my estimation.

To this day I can recall the hollow feelings I had as we landed. I was very, very far from my home, and in a strange land where not everyone was going to like us being there. Some would be hostile toward us, even wanting to kill us, and as a result we would scarcely be able to trust anyone. I may as well have been on a different planet or isolated on the moon. Even with all of the other guys around me, I nevertheless felt alone, filled with a copious dose of apprehension about what the future had in store for us. One thing was evident from the very beginning: all of us, including the enlisted ranks and commissioned officers, were in this together. *Were there enough of us here? How much backup did we really have?* All the risks we would take, and all the successes or failures we would endure, would be as a result of our functioning together as a single unit. One thing I never worried about was whether we were good enough to do whatever was required.

The thought crossed my mind that here I was, experiencing something that I would talk to my grandkids about someday. I never imagined that I would be in a situation such as this, nor be among the first from either of my hometowns to be over here. War was something old guys spoke of, if at all, not young plebes like me. I didn't have many friends to talk about this experience with, only the guys around me, and they were each absorbing this in their own way. We didn't know whether to expect a large enemy force making an attempt to overrun us or a single sniper taking aim at our helmets. All we knew was that either way we would be just as dead if the enemy was successful. I just wished that someone would come along and tell us how bad it was going to get. We were expected to suck up whatever happened and move forward. The inexperience and the unknown coupled together to work on our emotions. It was going to take some time and some interaction with the enemy forces before we could gauge how difficult our job was going to be.

We had landed near Chu Lai, South Vietnam, which is approximately fifty miles southeast of Da Nang, generally in the northern region of the country. To my knowledge, no American forces had ever landed at this particular spot. During the first few days we continued moving inland farther and farther away from the beach. Once a foothold was secured, we established an area of control from which to operate. Living conditions were primitive at best. We used our tarplike ponchos for keeping our butts dry and out of the dirt during the night. Ponchos are similar to tarps only with a hole and hood for your head. Later I would find that they were also the primary piece of gear that we would use for transporting casualties short distances. There were no litters available out here, like those we'd all seen in the war movies.

There really wasn't time to agonize about much of anything as we all had more than enough work to do. The workdays were long and as unrelenting as the heat from the sun, but we didn't really know what long days were yet. After the first couple of nights, we unfortunately experienced our first casualty, a fatality. It was a rainy and dark night, and everyone was jumpy, which I think was primarily due to our being in country for only a short time. There had also been some reports of enemy sightings and some brief sniper fire directed at us. This may have been the first time we were fired upon. I can't remember for certain.

The marines always established guard positions around the perimeter of the area under our control. These guys would encounter the enemy first and were the eyes and ears of our unit. The report back to us concerning the incident was that one of the platoon sergeants had been checking on his men who were on watch, making sure they all were awake and alert. In this instance he evidently and regrettably surprised the two young marines on guard duty from behind their position, who turned on him and fired. Someone commented that the sergeant thought that these men may have dozed off, but they had not. The platoon medical corpsman could do nothing, for the sergeant was killed instantly. The men involved were traumatized and in a state of shock over what had just happened. A full investigation eventually cleared them of wrongdoing, but they were rotated back to a rear area for further medical evaluations. No one talked much about this event, but it wasn't forgotten. People don't forget tragedies of this nature, especially those who have the misfortune of being involved. The older men appeared to take this as a matter of war, whereas we young guys couldn't believe that this had actually occurred. The sergeant epitomized what the Marine Corps was looking for in its noncommissioned officers. The end result was quick, permanent, totally unforgiving, and very sad.

C-Rations, which consisted of various canned foods all packaged tightly together inside one small cardboard box, were our primary source of meals. They contained items such as canned fruit, meat, fruitcake, pound cake, peanut butter, and crackers in addition to cocoa, coffee, toilet paper, a small pack of cigarettes, matches, and the world's smallest can opener. The cocoa was a good option, since I didn't drink much coffee then, and I regularly traded my pound cake for the canned fruit. I liked having the juice in the canned fruit since water was in short supply. I don't remember being able to trade my fruitcake for anything. Practically everyone smoked, and I was no exception ("Winston tastes good like a cigarette should"). Showers wouldn't be available for a while except when it rained, and we were happy just to have enough water to drink, let alone shave or brush our teeth. Not many days went by before we controlled the higher terrain, and as a result we established what would be our new home for a few weeks.

SEVEN

Digging In: Quick Glimpses of Hell

Our company spread out over a large hill, which offered an advantageous view of the beach far off in the distance, and also of the surrounding area closer in. Some of the guys would comment, "Vietnam may not be the rectum of the world, but you can see it from here." I believe this comment was directed more at the situation we found ourselves in, the ultraprimitive living conditions of the local people, and the weather as opposed to the overall quiet beauty of the terrain. This was basically just an abbreviated way of summarizing our state of affairs. Our fellow companies within the battalion located themselves on some of the other large hills in the area, thus dominating the high ground between the beach area and the inland pastures and rice paddies with their tiny villages. The marines worked their asses off during the day, digging out positions within the hillside to live in and to fight from if necessary. None of us had ever done this work back in the States.

The primary mission was to secure and protect the area parallel to the shoreline at Chu Lai so that a landing airstrip could be built along with a significant base of operations for a much larger military force in the future. Vegetation on our hill that might be useful for any type of cover or shade was virtually nonexistent. Our best friend, the poncho, configured into a lean-to of sorts was the only cover from the sun for the time being.

Food (C-Rations) and five-gallon water cans were delivered daily by helicopter, along with the very precious mail sack. Mail call was our only link to the world—that is, home. There were no cell phones, computers, or other avenues of communication available. Company attitudes could rise and fall on the availability and contents of the mail we received. When the mail sack did not arrive when expected, that was a real letdown, angering some and disappointing all.

Helicopters were indispensable for many reasons, but they were without a doubt more capable of creating a dust storm with their rotors than any dozen land vehicles combined, although the track vehicles such as a tank or M50 Ontos (a light armored track vehicle with six individual 106mm recoilless rifles mounted on top) could also kick up their share of dirt. I thought that the Ontos (Greek name for "thing") was particularly interesting from a design standpoint. The six rifles looked like six stovepipes mounted on top of a small tank. Even though we did not use them often, these vehicles were highly mobile and had sufficient firepower to support us if the situation warranted it.

The marines manually dug large bunkers deep in the hill and filled hundreds of sandbags with soil to build walls for what would be our shelter for a while. These larger bunkers were expansions of and in addition to the smaller ones mentioned above. These would be permanent, long-term structures strategically placed from which to defend ourselves. This activity was not done in one day or even a couple of weeks, but instead was an evolving process that resulted in us eventually having solid structures for protection and shelter. Large metal strips were used for constructing the Chu Lai airstrip runways. Darned if the marines didn't find a way to secure and transport a number of them via helicopter up to our hilltop. They were put to good use as overhead support structures upon which to lay more dirt-filled sandbags for added fortification. The bunkers prevented the midday sun from baking our skulls, provided us with a place to take cover from the occasional sniper fire, afforded a wide field of vision for observation purposes, and offered an excellent position from which to defend our hill in case of an attack. I dug and filled sandbags, but for the most part I merely lent a helping hand. They, in turn, found a spot for me inside one of the bunkers, of course.

Everyone had a job to do, either being assigned to a work party or as a part of their job responsibilities. When roles are defined, accomplishing the particular mission is much easier. No one expected me to help much with building bunkers, but they did expect me to be ready for any medical needs, which could arise at any time, including heat exhaustion, headaches, lacerations, sprains, and blisters, and we were ever watchful for heatstroke problems. Someone who was dry skinned and with a very high body temperature was in danger of losing consciousness and going into shock or worse if we couldn't cool them down fast enough. The best medicine for many of these ailments was prevention. Looking back, it seems as though we were in a state of constant heat exhaustion due to the daily high temperature and humidity. We couldn't carry enough water to stay properly hydrated during times of extreme exertion. A person could take a break while working on a bunker, but no break would be available if he were running down a trail in the middle of the day with numerous pounds of gear on his back, around his waist, and in his arms trying to chase down or take cover from an elusive enemy.

The guys were adept at stringing out the concertina wire around the base of our hill, and for additional protection they positioned Claymore antipersonnel mines in strategic locations near and within the wire, which created a potent deterrent for anyone attempting to breach our perimeter. The weather, while extremely hot, was pleasant and clear many of the nights. I often sat outside the bunker looking up at the night sky toward what I imagined was the direction of the United States, smoking a cigarette and wondering what was going on back home. I also wondered what was happening out there in the darkness surrounding our hill, which was an ever present reminder for me to make sure and cup my lit cigarette in my hands so that it wouldn't be a target. The lit end of a cigarette is visible from a long distance away, and if I wanted a cigarette outside, it needed to be kept from view as much as possible. Not only could I draw firepower to me, I could also put the guy sitting next to me in danger. Actually I became so used to cupping my cigarettes that I did it in the daytime out of habit.

Some nights there would be the rumble of large bombs exploding far off in the distance, usually to the north of where we were. More than likely they were dropped from our B-52s flying their bombing missions from high overhead. Overall it sounded like distant thunder, muffled but with almost kettle-drum-like precision, accompanied by synchronized flashes of light reflecting off the darkened horizon. It really did look and sound like hell on earth, even as far away as we were. Weeks from that point, I would have a firsthand opportunity to observe exactly how large of a crater these bombs made. I thank the Lord that I was never on the receiving end of anything even similar in magnitude.

During the dead of night someone on guard duty would periodically shoot up a flare to illuminate an area for improved visual scrutiny. Sending up a flare signaled the possibility that someone or something was attempting to move through the perimeter wire, but most of the time it was nothing more than an eerie, bright, and silent light illuminating the perimeter area, floating along over the hillside as it slowly drifted toward the ground. There was a distinctive aura at night as compared to the mood during the daylight hours. I think it was more a feeling of uneasiness due to the lack of visibility and not knowing what that night might bring. Chances were that the enemy was not going to advance on us during the daylight hours, but in the dark of night their options were appreciably better. Images in what little light was available could fool even the most experienced eyes, not to mention how an active imagination could invade rational thoughts and influence normal behavior. When repeated flares were lit, it generated an even higher alert level. We didn't yell down to those firing the flares, "Hey, what are you seeing down there?" Talking was minimal, and eyes were trained on whatever or whoever was out there. When someone did fire off a weapon during the night, all hell broke loose with a barrage of firepower until a cease-fire was ordered, which normally came very quickly, unless of course there was return fire from the enemy.

At about this time, one of our battalion sister companies, Golf Company, based on another hill, was attacked by a substantial Viet Cong force late one night. Although Golf Company overcame their attackers, they sustained moderate casualties in the process, which made us realize that it could just as easily have been us in this situation. The Viet Cong—commonly referred to as "Charlie" or "VC" (Victor Charlie)—were communist insurgents intermingling with those living in South Vietnam. They were also referred to as the National Liberation Front. Viet Cong might appear as civilian workers or farmers in the daytime, but during the night they essentially terrorized the small hamlets and the general population. They stole rice and killed anyone resisting them, including women and children.

The Viet Cong were primarily guerrilla fighters, although as I explain in later chapters, they could also engage with us via conventional warfare means if they had sufficient forces concentrated in a particular area. These are the enemy we thought we would encounter, as opposed to the North Vietnamese military itself. In the newspaper series about the Vietnam veterans I referred to earlier, one of the common themes was, "We never knew who the enemy was until they fired at us." Volumes of material about the Viet Cong are available for those wishing to learn more about their role and importance to the history of Vietnam.

There would be no warning. There was never an outright prediction of what the Viet Cong would or could attempt. The marines did a commendable job of making it a priority to never underestimate the potential for the enemy to harm us. The more time I spent with the marines under these conditions, the more respect I had for the way they approached their duties. I would not have admitted it back in Hawaii, but I know that I became a better hospital corpsman because of their commitment to always being prepared as much as possible. Their objective was to come out on top of any situation in which they found themselves. It would have been difficult back in a peaceful environment such as Hawaii for the marines to actually demonstrate their proficiency, but over here peace was rarely the norm.

From our vantage point, perched high upon these hills, we could observe the navy Seabees and various construction-engineering personnel operating their large earthmoving equipment to create what would soon become a fully functional airbase. Their efforts continued day and night, seven days a week. We also observed some of the large naval ships as they brought in the supplies and materials needed to support all of us. The airfield was actually developed far enough by June 1, 1965, for the first landing by an A-4 Skyhawk aircraft. The Marine Corps operated the Chu Lai Air Base from 1965 until 1970, at which time it was turned over to the US Army. Many times during those years the marines had to defend attacks from the Viet Cong as well as prevent attacks from ever materializing. The first major battle of the Vietnam War—Operation Starlite, discussed later—had very much to do with protecting our new base and airfield.

Later on I was fortunate to have an opportunity to proceed down to the airstrip with the hopes of locating one of my old school buddies from Kansas. He was in the Seabees and according to my parents was stationed at the Chu Lai airstrip. We did meet and had a brief but enjoyable visit there on the beach, miles from the wheat fields where we had attended school together. Visiting with him felt surreal, but for a moment, it shrank the world just a little, as Kansas came to Vietnam. It had been years since we had seen each other, but like when you meet up with a long-lost cousin, it didn't take long to get reacquainted. I saw him again many years later at my father's funeral. We didn't have much of a chance to talk at that time either, but I know we each felt good seeing that both of us had made a good life for ourselves in the years after Vietnam.

My typical day included making rounds along with my platoon corpsmen, speaking with the marines, and conducting routine medical examinations. Taking good care of the feet was of paramount importance. Blisters, cuts, or any other sores could easily become infected in these conditions and compound the problem into a much more serious medical issue if not prevented and treated effectively. Foot care might not have been the most exciting medical subject to deal with, but it may have been the most important. Everywhere we went, at least within a five-mile radius, we walked, in dry and wet conditions. Wading through muddy water and rice paddies, having rain-soaked clothes, including boots and socks, and then walking in this clothing until it dried on its own was not uncommon. No change of clothes was readily available. Any one of us would have given any amount of money to be able to take a shower.

It may not be the appropriate medical treatment today, but in those days everyone was supposed to consume a specific quantity of salt tablets daily. As I indicated earlier, heat exhaustion or heatstroke occurred rapidly, especially during the daytime. Even though I kept my eye on the guys for any indications they were heading in this direction, it was more important for them to know what to look for, before it was too late. They were educated in the symptoms and the proper things to do, providing there was water available and someone wasn't shooting at you.

There wasn't a way I could watch all of them all of the time. Such issues were due in part to the amount of gear that we hauled on our backs, around our waists, and over the shoulders, in addition to the protective flak jacket we might be wearing. If that wasn't enough, there was always that ten-pound piss pot on our head, which may have helped with shrapnel but was of little use in stopping or deflecting bullets. There is nothing like running around in the heat of the day with a bouncing and frequently tilting helmet that felt too big to wear but too small to hide under. No one wanted to test the hypothesis of our helmet being able to stop a bullet, but we all wore them all the time while out on patrols. I admit that I probably could have adjusted the headband and chin strap of my helmet to stay on better. I also have to admit that on those occasions when I did not have to wear the helmet, I felt a bit naked.

The majority of our patrols and excursions into the surrounding countryside were carried out at night. During the day, work was performed on the bunkers, such as adding more sandbags. Weapons were cleaned, and the marines had other chores to do. Someone had to burn out the toilets and receive the chow and mail, in addition to performing guard duty. There were days that were boring but never relaxing. One fateful day, without any warning, a short-round artillery shell (one that doesn't make it to its target) landed directly in a small, sandbagged, open-top bunker with three or four men sitting in it. I don't remember if their bunker was finished yet or if we hadn't yet received the large metal strips to use for the rooftops. Dust and dirt were in the air everywhere, and by the time I ran up to where the men were, it looked as if they had been lifted up then put back down by the blast from the artillery round. They were sitting up against some of the sandbags in an almost natural pose. The difference was that they were lifeless and covered in dust and dirt, and their faces were chalky white and expressionless. The immediate area had the sickening odor of gunpowder—a rotten-egg, sulfuric smell, which is the only way I know how to describe it. Some of them had chunks of their bodies missing as if something had ripped a part of them out of their own torsos. They had all been killed instantly in this misfit of circumstance.

I did all I could to maintain my composure in front of their buddies and others who had gathered around us trying to help in any way possible. I didn't even know what the hell I was looking for. I had not seen that many dead people before, especially those who had just been killed five minutes ago. I had spoken with some of these men a short time earlier, and now they were gone with a finality and swiftness that was very difficult to accept. We carefully and respectfully transferred them out of the bunker and prepared them for transport by helicopter off of their hill. I had a difficult time wrestling with the fact that our own weapons did this. I kept thinking that there must be a better way to accomplish the same thing, and what a tragedy this was for these young men, their buddies on the hill that day, and of course their families back home. Did they have to fire the artillery directly over us to reach the target? Could they have located the artillery so that it fired over the side of our hill? As fate would have it, I would experience another encounter with short rounds during my tour of duty in Vietnam. Thus far, I had treated more casualties due to our own misfortunes than from enemy attacks.

Incidents such as these are referred to as "casualties by friendly fire." What an oxymoron! I remember thinking about the day's events that night, along with the smell of gunpowder lingering in my nostrils. I had never liked the sound of artillery rounds whistling over our heads. Now I know why, even though I realized the necessity of possessing heavy weapons support. Their unnatural sound passing overhead had instilled yet another fear of the unknown and uncontrollable course of events that likely would happen when least expected. Those live artillery rounds passing over our heads were another one of those situations that couldn't be practiced in Hawaii. I don't think that I would have forgotten the experience. I will never forget this one.

Over the next couple of months our company maintained control on and around the hilly terrain we inhabited. During the night, small, squad-sized patrols (eight to ten men) made short probes into the surrounding countryside, setting up ambush sites until daylight arrived. Typically, a single medical corpsman accompanied the squads on these missions, and I got in on my share of them. Normally there was not much action on the patrols; however, on more than one occasion it had crossed my mind that I was out here in the middle of nowhere with only a handful of marines. Here we were, away from the protection of the command post on our hill, except for radio contact, not knowing what we would encounter in the dead of night. The senior person leading these night missions was normally a corporal with some experience as a squad leader, and they did a good job of keeping everyone in line and on track to accomplish the primary objective. One thing is certain. If I would have had to lead the squad back to our home base, we would have been screwed, since I was not trained in map reading or in the correct procedures for successfully engaging the enemy. All we could do was to make sure we had plenty of ammo.

One dark but otherwise quiet night on one of these patrols after we had just settled in, a young marine yelled out that he had been bitten by a snake. I scrambled over to him in the dark and carefully focused a light on his injury, which happened to be on his neck. He didn't actually see the snake or feel the snake, but that was understandable. Sure enough, there were two small marks spaced apart just as a snakebite might look. *How many snakebites had I seen before?* I asked myself. The answer was not many: none to be exact. *What now?* My experience in dealing with snakebites was nonexistent. I couldn't apply a tourniquet around his neck to slow the circulation of the poison if it actually was a snakebite. Even if the bite were on one of his limbs, applying a tourniquet to slow the circulation of the poison was a procedure requiring close monitoring because incorrect use of a tourniquet could do more damage to the patient. I wasn't going to make an incision between the marks and suck the poison out. I don't believe that this was an approved procedure even then, and I would not be making cuts on his neck in any case. In the time I had been in Vietnam I had not seen any snakes, but occasionally there were scorpions observed running around on the ground. The patient's vital signs were good, his pupils normal, no swelling by the bite, and he was experiencing no respiratory problems. I decided to clean up the bite area on his neck with an antiseptic, give him some painkillers, keep him still, and stay close by his side, maintaining a close eye on him during the night. He was not overly excited by the experience, but he was concerned, as was I, that neither of us knew for sure what exactly had happened.

Many times as we patrolled directly through or on the edges of these tiny rural villages, we could see the Vietnamese families in their primitive homes, gathered around a fire, eating their evening meal. In all probability it consisted of a bowl of rice with possibly some vegetables, and maybe some small amounts of meat. There were no glass windows, doors, or sewer systems, let alone electricity. More likely than not, positioned directly alongside their home was the family's water buffalo tucked away in its pen. When one of these animals snorts at you or shakes his head while looking at you, it has a tendency to grab your attention, particularly if you hadn't noticed this large beast in the darkness. The Vietnamese people were highly dependent on the family water buffalo for their livelihood. This animal was their tractor, as it were, and it performed a wide variety of tasks together with its master, toiling in the rice fields from dawn to dusk. It was a serious infraction, and depending upon the circumstances, a punishable offense to injure or kill one of these creatures without provocation.

On these small nightly operations I was always happy to see dawn appear. This meant we could eat something before we dragged our weary butts back to base camp for the day. Hopefully nothing was going on that would prevent us from catching a few *z*'s. The marine who was bitten by something at the ambush site checked out fine back at the battalion aid station, and he had no further medical problems related to whatever had occurred the previous night. I wasn't totally surprised at this outcome, but I was relieved that he was going to be all right since I actually did not know what caused the marks on his neck.

One of the aims of this narrative is to provide the reader with a flavor and a cross-section of the various types of activities that we took part in while we were guests of South Vietnam. We were getting involved up to our chinstraps in an expanding conflict, if not a war, as we were occasionally reminded. It was not a declared war, but over time and in the literature it seems "war" is the term used most often. I was never worried back then about the nomenclature associated with what we were doing over there, and I'm not today. The search-and-destroy operations ranged in scope and manpower from the squad-sized patrols discussed above to platoon- or company-level operations in terms of power, and large-scale battalion or even multibattalion campaigns. Bits and pieces of many encounters and undertakings come to mind, but I believe the examples presented will enable the reader to have a detailed impression of what it took to carry out our duties. Hopefully the reader will also embrace a heightened sense of awareness regarding the high costs sustained by our country.

One evening a couple of platoons from our unit embarked upon an operation led by the company commander (captain) himself. We started our trek at sunset and all during the night we traversed through pastureland and creeks and along the rice paddies in full battle gear with helmets, and even flak jackets, which were a real pain in the butt to deal with. The flak jacket was heavy, hot, and awkward to wear, in addition to making every movement that much more difficult. However, it might also save my life under the right circumstances. I remember the weather being hot as hell, and as we were leaving the area we snaked by a battery of artillery (howitzers) firing off round after round into the evening sky. They were shoving the shells in these big guns and disposing of the empty shell casings as fast as they could by the way it appeared to me. The sound was deafening, and the ground shook from the recoil action. Being with an infantry company, it was a new experience for many of us to see this work taking place up close and personal.

One of the many habits that I had developed being a part of the armed forces was to compare my job with those of other personnel. After all, it was my first real full-time, year-round job. I remember thinking to myself that maybe these guys didn't have to walk a lot and be exposed to some of the immediate danger that we were, but without a doubt they did have to work their asses off. I'm sure the misery index was high, taking into account their working conditions, with all the noise and heat from the shells going off, the weather, not to mention their having to lift the heavy rounds until their arms probably felt like rubber. I believe I correctly came to the instantaneous conclusion that I would stay with my present job . . . as if I had a choice in the matter anyway.

Up until now I wasn't sure that it was possible to sleep and walk at the same time, but I think just about all of us with the exception of the captain did some of this during our nightly march. I know I bumped into the guy ahead of me on more than one occasion, particularly if we suddenly stopped, and the guy behind me did the same thing. My mind drifted off toward home, as it often did, when I would daydream on these patrols. Such brief, self-induced excursions took me away from the miserable reality of my surroundings. It was not a wise thing to become complacent, so these little mental escapes out of Vietnam had to occur at well-chosen times. Everyone still had to maintain some level of alertness, even though any one of us would have given a day's pay to simply stop and catch a few winks or eat something. Each of us had worked a normal day before we embarked on this impromptu operation, and this made the night seem even longer than it really was.

We proceeded in this manner until dawn, at which time we stopped to have a quick meal of C-Rations before heading back to base camp. Evidently this was more of a reconnaissance patrol than anything else, because we hadn't encountered any resistance to this point. Maybe the captain was putting us through some sort of endurance test so that we would be better prepared for what lay ahead. Maybe he was pissed at us for some reason, but I don't think so. No one asked, and he didn't offer an explanation. There was another world of intelligence gathering and communications higher up the chain of command deciding where we would go and what we would do. It didn't have to make sense to the rank and file. My thought was, *Just don't take me on any more joyrides.*

As we were in the initial stages of returning back to base we came upon an area that had been booby-trapped. We had earlier noticed that there were punji stakes in the area, which are sharpened bamboo stakes that are implanted into the ground with their pointed end facing up toward anyone who might fall or step on them. They were likely tipped with fecal material and were embedded along the sides of our trail. Their primary purpose was to injure or kill anyone who either fell or dove onto them while attempting to take cover in the ditches during a firefight. Dipping them in feces increased the odds of developing a serious infection if injured by one of them. We had learned about their possible use from our earlier training in Hawaii. I didn't see them often, but they were an ominous reminder that our enemy was both creative and versatile in expressing hatred of us in a clear manner. "All is fair in love and war, and this most assuredly wasn't love."

The booby traps were set out in open pastureland that appeared harmless enough at first glance, but one misstep could send any one of us home in a body bag or back to the hospital missing a limb. I wouldn't have known what a booby trap looked like even if it were positioned directly in my path, except from the standpoint that by its appearance it would not be a naturally occurring item in this environment. The point man was trained not only to look for these traps, but he and others knew how to detonate them as well. This was one job that I wouldn't trade with for all the tea in South Vietnam. I wondered, *Why couldn't we simply walk around this area?* but that was not to be. These traps had to be located and destroyed not just for our benefit but for the protection of any friendlies or civilians coming that way. I didn't think about it at the time, but it was a good message to send to the ingenious vermin who set the booby traps that it didn't work out too well for them this time around.

Cautiously, I followed the footprint from the guy in front of me as much as possible. Step by step in single file we wound our way along in this manner for what seemed like an eternity. I mentally questioned, *What would I do if my services were needed up at the front of the line? How could I get up there without endangering everyone else and myself?* Each of us was waiting for something to happen, but at the same time we had confidence in those at the front of the line who were cautiously examining and probing our route. A few times we paused; someone yelled, "Fire in the hole!"; and a booby trap was detonated. It was likely either a mine or a grenade. I was glad when they destroyed one of these traps, but it certainly added to the reality of the situation. I didn't get close enough to see exactly what the Viet Cong had left for us. The marines in front also checked out and blew the entrances shut to some underground tunnels the enemy had made for their use. These entrances looked primitive and nothing at all like a hole in the ground that I would even think about crawling into.

Every step I took was carefully navigated, and I thought about how good it would feel to get beyond this crap. When the all-clear signal was given so that we could proceed in a normal fashion, my first inclination was to bend down and kiss the precious ground. I remember making a mental decree at that time that, if I had a choice, I would much rather be shot at than endure this walking-on-eggs scenario again. Later, I would need to reevaluate this declaration. I thanked the Good Lord that I didn't have to treat anyone for a booby-trap injury, and once again I think that the training and skills these marines, especially those guys on point, had, paid off in spades for all of us that day.

This experience was more than a little unnerving. I think the primary reason it bothered me, besides the serious damage the booby traps potentially caused, was the feeling of being helpless. We couldn't have even run for cover. There was nothing to fire back at or even scare away. We did eventually get back to base camp later that day, which, I'll have to concede, looked darned good.

Not all of our work was of a hostile or an unpleasant nature. From time to time we visited some of the larger communities within the area and conducted medical clinics, normally at the local schools. The Vietnamese people brought their children to have their scratches and sores cleaned and dressed or to have us medically check the whole family over, if they were comfortable with what they saw us doing. Sometimes a battalion doctor accompanied us, and together the medical personnel along with the marines all participated in what amounted to a goodwill gesture for military-civilian public relations. There was nothing like seeing an oversized jarhead smiling ear to ear and passing out candy to dirty little hands grabbing what they could for all their worth, a little like Halloween back home. "Jarhead" is a nickname given to the marines because of their short haircuts, among other things. They have actually taken ownership of the name and refer to themselves as jarheads in a positive association.

The only difference from Halloween back home was that these children probably had never in their lives seen or had much in the way of treats. It warmed our hearts to see their little faces with their big brown eyes, no shoes, rags for clothes, little in the way of good hygiene, and possessing absolutely nothing of material worth, smiling in appreciation of even the smallest thing they received. I know it did all of us some good to actually be performing work that at least resembled normal human activities. These children were certainly not to blame for any of the misery and turmoil that was around them and their families every day. From what I could tell, they didn't have *anything*.

Along the sides of the main road leading into these towns were small tin shanties, sometimes with a hammock and always a dirt floor. This was about all that any of them had for shelter. No one was noticeably any better off than the next person, and there was a stark similarity in their facial expressions, which I would describe as an ever-enduring hopelessness. In reality, I don't think they were as well off as the very rural Vietnamese people, who at least had work to do and food to eat. I'm not sure these people had either. They were living under these conditions long before we had landed, and unfortunately things would not improve fast enough for many of them. Someday if we were lucky, we knew that we had a ride home waiting for us. What did these people have to look forward to? We didn't really have a clue. They needed much more than a few bars of soap, candy treats for the children, and elemental medical care.

On one occasion while we were in town, I decided to get a haircut. As I sat in the chair waiting for the barber to sharpen his straight razor for trimming my neck line, I thought to myself, *Is this really a good idea?* There really was no safe zone, and the prevailing belief was that literally anyone around us could be Viet Cong, even though this town was approved for us to spend limited time in and visit. I think that this feeling was only amplified by the fact that the language barrier was huge. We could not understand what they were saying, nor they us. When we were treating the sick people, we had to work hard at making sure we knew what their medical complaint was. I didn't feel threatened while we conducted the sick calls for the townspeople. This may have been due to the situation: they needed us to help them.

The barber evidently was not a VC sympathizer, because I received a good haircut, he made a profit, and I felt a little more like a human being once again. I did make sure that one of my corpsman buddies was in the barber shop at all times while I was getting my hair cut, and I did the same for him. I'm not sure who was protecting whom, but it made us feel better even if we may have been fooling ourselves just a little.

Our first few months in Vietnam were spent gaining experience not only in adapting to our habitats and living conditions physically and mentally but in becoming more and more confident in what we were doing. No one was acting salty yet, but we were becoming less and less jumpy. Thus far, our combat action had been largely confined to occasional sniper fire or landing zone resistance when we launched an operation using helicopters. These sporadic clashes were normally snuffed out by the superior firepower from our forces before they could expand into lengthy firefights.

Even though we were becoming more self-assured, situations still occurred that resulted in less than ideal consequences. There was an instance during a platoon-sized patrol where an enemy suspect wearing the familiar black pajama clothing was observed running away along a rice paddy dike down the hillside far down in the flatlands from where we were located. We had experienced enemy contact at about this same period of time, so the order was given to stop this person. Our guys hit their target, and we proceeded toward the location where the enemy casualty lay. There were other excited and agitated local people gathered around by this time, and in short order we realized that the wounded person was an elderly woman. I don't know if she was an insurgent sympathizer or not, but I felt no threat from her and proceeded to treat her wounds and comfort her without knowing how to communicate with her, except through eye contact, touch, and my own actions. After we calmed her down, she was transported by helicopter to our medical facilities.

Technically she may have been a suspect because of her attire (black pajamas are what the Viet Cong were known for) and identification materials, but everyone was surprised to see who was lying on the ground writhing in pain. It was common knowledge that children and women were used for gathering information about our forces, and were even used as decoys and weapons carriers. They reportedly could drop a grenade in a crowd of our guys, smiling at them as they did so. Even knowing this information I had no apprehension about the people we treated at the makeshift clinics, as I mentioned earlier. It was apparent that not many of us looked upon this current action as a positive event. I have no idea what the follow-up investigation concluded, but even with our own safety always as the top priority, I had the impression that most everyone there thought that we could have handled this better. The local people would agree, I'm quite certain.

EIGHT

Happy Twenty-First Birthday: Operation Starlite on the Horizon

Until this point, many of us still had a dimming yet flickering notion that we would be going back to the "world" (the United States) any day now, especially since the airstrip was coming along well. There was still no established tour of duty, or at least not one that was conveyed to us. We were hopeful that we would be in Vietnam a few months, just temporarily, until the US Army would take over operations on a permanent basis. The marines, after all, were the initial strike force of a military operation until the army could take over on a permanent basis, or so we always thought. I don't remember our basis for this belief, but at this point in time no one was talking about a protracted Vietnam War but rather the Vietnam conflict in which we were assisting the people of South Vietnam. We were there to help the South Vietnamese military and its citizens overcome the Viet Cong insurgents and defend against any military troops coming in from communist North Vietnam. I had no idea if all of this was correct, but we were there to help the South Vietnamese and protect our own interests. I had no reason to doubt this, but I wondered if our effort was worth it. Other than the normal bitching that all marines do, I didn't hear a lot of questioning among the men about our mission.

Eventually, after a few months, we did receive word that we would be staying in Vietnam for a while. It was always a case of, "If we don't hear anything official about leaving, then we are staying for as long as it takes. Don't worry about it." I guess it was sort of a need-to-know attitude for information sharing.

The United States was rapidly building up troop numbers in the country, not lessening them, so obviously no one would be going home anytime soon. It wasn't as if the South Vietnamese government said, "Thank you for all your help. We can handle it from here." A normal tour of duty became thirteen months (rotating to stateside during the thirteenth month), and that was the fact of it. In retrospect it would have been better for morale to have established and communicated this information early on. At least all of the new personnel coming into Vietnam knew beforehand what their tour would be, so they knew what to expect and plan for in terms of a time frame. Since we were among the first combat units in Vietnam, it is understandable that a tour of duty was not established, but like most anything else, it could have been done better. In the military, one doesn't really have much in the way of input about anything, especially regarding how to spend one's time. Ironically, the thing most people, especially during their first enlistment, cared more about than anything else was time, and I certainly was no exception. I believe that it ties in with freedom, which, for the present, we all had lost temporarily. There were those old feelings of resentment toward the military draft, which at least in an indirect sense influenced why most of us were sitting here. At least it was a good excuse, in our eyes.

It had been raining for days on end, or so it seemed. Someone said that we were in the monsoon season, and for all I knew, they were correct. One miserable night in particular, I remember we were out on patrol, hunkered down against a rice paddy dike with our boots anchored in the stinking rice paddy water and glue-like mud. Like everyone else, I covered myself with my poncho in an attempt to stay dry and not get so wet that I stank from my own salt-stained and sweat-ridden clothing. We were set in place for the night, and here I was, turning twenty-one years of age on this rain-soaked bitch of a July evening. *No self-respecting Viet*

8.1 My young self—I think I was in Chu Lai. Courtesy of H. Krentel, fellow hospital corpsman

Cong would be out in conditions like this, I figured, but there would be no birthday cheer this evening. My mind was primed for one of those little mental side trips, pondering what the future might look like once I was out of here and back in civilian life. After all, I was almost in my fourth year of a four-year active-duty enlistment. I would be a short-timer—soon to be getting out of the military–in a few months. Getting out of the military, at least off active duty, was the recurrent focus whether in private thought or shooting the bull with my buddies. For the whole world to witness, I was legally an adult now, and by the grace of God I would be able to vote and do all the things accorded to twenty-one-year-olds back in the United States, if I made it out of Vietnam. Hell of a deal, if I'd have been in a position to celebrate. What a pisser this was!

Twenty-one or not, my relationships with members of the opposite sex up until that point were on the restricted side of the playboy sliding scale (not exactly an experienced playboy), and I sure as hell didn't want to die in my status quo out in the middle of these dung-ridden rice paddies. I had a clear ambition to sow a few wild oats before being sniped by some lucky-shot Viet Cong "Charlie Boy Gook." Yes, we referred to them as "gooks," particularly when emotions were running high. It's not something to be proud of, but to say there were no such remarks would be a lie, and this was the enemy we were talking about . . . the majority of the time anyway. During the night I visualized going to college one day and having my own family to support after I graduated and had acquired a good job. I remember this as being an extraordinarily long night that wore on and on, and a night during which I got soaked to the bone despite all of my preparations. I had no way of knowing what the future would hold, but somehow I knew that my life was not going to end out here. The next morning, I was very much alive and twenty-one years old, a milestone to me at least, and I only had to survive from mid-July until May of the next year. Here I was, twenty-one today, and not a bar in sight. Of course I had no way to foresee that things were about to change for the worse, and that we would all age considerably in the months ahead, those of us who would still be present and accounted for, that is.

As I recall, at about this time in our tour of duty, we moved down from the hill into an area where we had large multiperson tents and even a small mess tent where hot food was prepared. I could also walk to the battalion aid station to get supplies and on occasion see some of my fellow corpsmen from back in Hawaii. I'm not sure of the reason for our relocation. Except for looking out over the land from the hilltop, I was not complaining. We still carried out patrols in the more immediate area, and frequently we would take a ride on the helicopters. It was on a small night patrol that one of my platoon corpsman shot one of the enemy in the head with his pistol. The Viet Cong had apparently walked right into where the squad he was with had set up an ambush site. This particular corpsman was one of the most polite and quiet men with whom I had ever worked. The enemy was no doubt in very close proximity to him. The corpsman didn't want to talk about the incident, but his platoon sure looked up to him in admiration.

The first major military operation of the war was about to take place. Unknown to myself at the time, this was a multibattalion, highly secret operation—including amphibious forces—that was planned and under the command of US Marine Corps General L. Walt, who had experience in both World War II and Korea. He and others scripted the battle plan to counter a large and organized attack set to occur very soon by the Viet Cong insurgents against our forces at Chu Lai. Evidently they were intent on destroying the airstrip, which no doubt was a major problem for them. The operation was dubbed "Operation Starlite," and it commenced for our battalion on August 18, 1965. After fifty years, many of the specific details blur together in my memory, and there are gaps in the flow of things as they occurred. However, much of what went on that day is with me forever.

Prior to the start of this large and critical operation, we assembled within an open yet secured area for our ensuing deployment by helicopter the next morning. As I remember, it was rainy and damp, and the impending mission was on all of our minds. There weren't many particulars provided, but it sounded as if we were about to engage a sizable and well-armed enemy force. None of us were looking forward to it, but we were ready to do the job we had come all this way to do and that we trained to do. We were going to be a part of something unknown to most of us, and it was pretty clear that this action was going to be more intense than what we had been involved in up to that point. Later I would read historical accounts stating that there were at least a couple of thousand Viet Cong, including some of their best mortar units, gathered together in the Quang Ngai Province region that was our destination.

We also realized that some of us would not be coming back, but we didn't talk about it. The officers and senior enlisted personnel probably discussed potential casualties as part of their planning, but on the troop level there really was no point, because we sure as hell couldn't do anything about it. The term "conflict" does not accurately describe what was about to occur over the next couple of days. Be assured that no one was thinking about saving South Vietnam this evening but rather of self-preservation and survival. This meant not having our bodies ripped apart by shrapnel or bullets, and not eating dirt or dying from wounds inflicted by a faceless enemy hidden behind whatever cover they could find. There was no escape, no quitting, no going back, and no way to move but forward. It was going to be one of those nights when no one rests well. I imagine that all battles begin with tired souls. Marines are very adept at not overreacting, and they resourcefully accommodate the worst of conditions, but any one of them who claimed they were not scared that night was lying to both himself and his fellow comrades. This action was going to be different from sniper fire and the small, short-lived firefights we had seen to date. I tried my best to get some sleep, but like many of the others it seemed that I wanted to jam in all the good thoughts from back home that I could—while I had the chance.

It was a short night that made it seem as if I had been cheated out of my sleep, but in no time we were up, eating our C-Rations, and I was probably drinking a big canteen cup of hot chocolate. It would soon be time to saddle up—to get off our asses and, with our gear, move to one of the staging areas where we would board one of the many helicopters that were flying in, then taking off one right after the other. This would occur after last-minute inspections of our equipment, weapons, and all other gear were made and then checked once more. The sergeants and other noncommissioned officers were relentless and thorough in having everyone make sure they had what they were supposed to have on their person. Once in a while they'd even look my way and say, "Everything okay with you, Doc?" to which I answered in the affirmative. I felt good that they were thinking of me, too, because I was damned sure thinking of them.

Everything was all business now. It was a sight to see as one by one the helicopters followed each other in an almost identical pattern of landing, boarding, then lifting, and flying forward yet dropping down as if we were going to scrape the ground, before eventually one by one it was up and away. "Getting it on" wasn't a phrase yet in those days, but that is what we all wanted to do: "get it on and get it over with," especially the "get it over with" part. I think our eyes, including my own, were probably a little more wide open than normal this morning. I know in my case I was scared, but not terrified, of almost everything that I had to look forward to this day. I accepted it emotionally, but there was no way I could predict how I would respond for sure. That would be determined on how bad it got and my own personal strengths.

Standing and waiting for a helicopter was nothing new to us. The vast majority of the time, our nonwalking mode of transportation was by helicopter. The chopper of choice for our use resembled a grasshopper, due to its large front windows and overall appearance. The Huey model helicopter, commonly seen in movies about Vietnam, was used for medical evacuations some of the times, but we rode the slower grasshoppers to and from our destinations. The Huey choppers didn't hold as many of us, and I had the impression that there were not high numbers of them available in the early days of the war, at least in the Marine Corps. Many times during takeoff our helicopter seemed to barely clear the treetops on the perimeter of the landing zones as we slowly lifted up and away for parts unknown. I liked to ride along with my legs dangling out of the doorway, my right hand firmly on the grab bar, while sitting directly across the open doorway from the machine-gunner position. I wanted this spot, not because I was brave or some kind of a daredevil, but because I wanted to be the first or second guy off the chopper when we hit the landing zone. I didn't want to be there sitting in the chopper, especially in a "hot LZ" (landing zone under enemy fire). They drilled into us during the training at Camp Pendleton, "He who hesitates is lost." I remembered and heeded those words every day of my tour. It was critically important to not only be attentive to your surroundings but to act alertly. We were trained to take care of ourselves at all times.

The actions and some of the forces at work that I observed both within and outside of the helicopter were interesting, especially as we drew closer and closer to the drop-off point. Frequently, I would see small white puffs of smoke from the small-arms fire, and if I wasn't on the first chopper to land, I could see the colored smoke from the smoke grenades that were used to mark and show wind direction at the landing zone for the rest of us to approach. I didn't worry much about the Viet Cong shooting at our helicopters until the day that a bullet found its way through the floor, grazing one of our guys by his ear. At some moments when we were descending, the machine gunner would swing his M-60 around and fire back and forth, traversing those areas that he thought were the sources of enemy fire. At these points, my anxiety level increased exponentially.

Looking toward the front of the chopper I could see the boots of the pilot and copilot move the various pedal-like devices up and down, performing their prelanding tasks as they came in to the landing zone. I'm not qualified to judge their piloting skills, but they were good enough for me! When the machine gunner said, "Go," we jumped off the bird as fast as we could, whether it was down on the ground or merely suspended near it. All of us ran for cover just as we were trained to do. All of us were spread out to maximize our influence on whatever we had to deal with, and to minimize ourselves as targets. Heads down and hunched over, and never running directly behind the helicopter were words to live by since the blades and rear rotor were not far off the ground. If we were being fired upon during the landing, which was commonplace, the marines immediately engaged the enemy, and I readied myself to provide medical aid as needed.

Sometimes after we had jumped off the choppers, I looked back as they became airborne again, disappearing into the distance. I was thankful that they made it out okay. I was temporarily envious that the crew would probably be sleeping that evening on a nice clean cot in a tent back in the rear, far away from the action. On the other hand, I wouldn't have traded places with any one of them. They returned to the hostile areas over and over again, appearing as large sitting ducks, even if for only a short time, and having absolutely no place to hide while we got on or off of them. They were slow and deliberate in their own right, and most certainly they were no match for the velocity of the rifle bullets being fired at them. Sitting in the landing zones for any length of time was not an option. Later I would get a close, firsthand look at how brave these helicopter crews actually were, as they repeatedly flew in and out of the landing areas under very hostile conditions, transporting casualties to the rear for advanced medical care. I would much rather take my chances of having the freedom to move around and hopefully not make myself an easier target than I already was. While the grass always looks a little greener on the other side of the fence, I was beginning to learn to appreciate what I had. I heard on more than one occasion that the most dangerous job in combat was that of radioman, and the second most dangerous was hospital corpsman. It was believed that if they were killed, the unit would be functionally harmed overall due to the nature of their work. I'm not sure these statements are accurate since all jobs in combat are dangerous. I never worried, because I was in good hands if it was true or not.

"Get on, go!" was the simple command. We boarded the helicopters just as we had done many times before in our training and in Vietnam. There was no hesitation or stumbling around trying to change anything or do anything different. We were ready, and that is the way it should be. As I look back after all these years, it still amazes me how methodical we were in going about our business that morning as we began Operation Starlite.

It was a short and quiet trip to the landing zone, but the LZ was intermittently hot, and we headed for cover once we were out of our helicopter. It was chaotic with all the choppers coming in almost on top of one another, yelling and shouting of orders, and everyone moving in what seemed like all directions. Figure 8.2 shows some of the helicopters coming in behind the one that had just dropped off those men on the ground. One of the main things I wanted to make sure to do is to stay with my unit and not get lost in the turmoil. My job was to always go where they went and not get left behind or not be available should I be needed. In short, I needed to keep my eyes open and stay watchful to what was going on around me, even if I didn't necessarily grasp it all.

Echo Company got organized, and we geared up for what was going to be a day none of us would soon forget. It didn't take very long before "Corpsman, corpsman" was heard from a short distance away from where I was located. Now my heart was pounding out of my chest. Crouched over, I ran to where I was needed—pumped up, but doing my level best to look calm and deliberate about what I was doing. At this point no bullets were flying directly overhead or in my vicinity. I thought, *What would my guys' confidence in me be if I were a shaky Jake and looked like I was about ready to lose my breakfast?* I may have felt like I was going to be sick, but it could never show.

My first casualty of the day was a captured Vietnamese enemy suspect who had been stabbed directly in his ass with a bayonet. There wasn't a great deal of blood coming from his puncture wound, but I

8.2 Echo Company Helicopter; Beginning of Operation Starlite.
Courtesy of Tim Page

securely applied a battle dressing—pressure—to keep it clean and to mitigate any additional hemorrhaging. He was in distress and hurting by the expression on his face, and he understandably was crying out in pain. I didn't feel threatened by him or any of his actions, but then again I didn't know the circumstances of why he was stabbed. He appeared to calm down a bit once I had his wound tended to, and he seemed to be aware that no one was going to do him any further harm. I recruited three volunteers on the spot, and the four of us, using a poncho for a stretcher, carried him to one of our helicopters for medical evacuation out of the area.

Little did I realize it at the beginning of the day, but there was at least one photojournalist embedded with us on the operation. Much later I found out that a picture of us carrying my Vietnamese patient to the med-evacuation helicopter was included in the September 3, 1965, issue of *LIFE* magazine (see Figure 8.3). There were other pictures from Operation Starlite in this issue, including Figure 8.2. These images were taken at great personal risk by Tim Page from Australia. This publication was probably the most widely read and well-known periodical avail-

8.3 First Casualty of the Day Operation Starlite. Captured Prisoner. Courtesy of Tim Page

able at the time. I came to know of this picture in a letter from my mom and dad, asking, "Is this you?" My parents didn't subscribe to *LIFE*, but someone in my little hometown back in Nebraska evidently had wondered about it and asked them. I don't know how these people made the connection to me from what was in the article, unless they somehow knew my military unit.

In my letters home I made it a point never to write about what happened in the field, so that my family wouldn't have to constantly worry about my well-being, although my sister and younger brother told me years later that it was very difficult for both Mom and Dad. Now it was too late for any preventive measures, because the article in the magazine was a featured spread, and it was largely accurate in both word and illustration. I don't believe my parents or brothers and sister were ever fooled about what I was involved in, and I was upset that this article appeared the way it did. Nevertheless, I continued to make it a point not to write about the more gruesome details about the war, but rather about things less dramatic. Sometimes I had to be a little creative to find the words. The odd thing is that I am not even recognizable in the photo, because it was taken of our backs and sides primarily, and the only person whose face is clearly shown was that of the Vietnamese man being loaded in the helicopter, which was definitely recognizable to me. I learned many years later from my youngest brother, who was home at the time, that Mom knew exactly which person I was in the picture. When he asked her how she knew that, she said, "I just know." She was absolutely correct, as possibly only a mom could have been. (I'm on the far left side.)

That day there would be no time to dwell on what had occurred only minutes ago. There was heavy small-arms fire coming from the ridges directly in front of us and off to our sides, as we proceeded over some smaller hills toward the base of a large hill we were preparing to ascend. I recall that I did not have a real clear perspective on where everyone was or what exactly was going on as the marines returned fire with considerably more force than the enemy. Even so, the enemy fire was not quieted permanently as it was when we dealt with snipers. The marines moved on during the times that I stopped to treat casualties, and it took me a while to readjust to what was taking place around me after each stop. I didn't need to know what the big picture was, but I did need to get to where I was needed and not lose track of where people were. During the numerous exchanges of firepower, the enemy rounds didn't stop coming or even quiet down except for brief pauses. This alone was intimidating, because it implied a greater level of peril than we had experienced to date.

In truth it was mass chaos, with orders and commands shouted over the gunfire. Conditions were very loud, yet overall there were elements of control and organization in terms of our forces moving forward and accomplishing their objectives a portion at a time. All of the noise and commotion from the firefights elevated everyone to peak levels of anxiety and emotion. If it were possible to closely examine the real-time activities individually, we no doubt would find each person enduring their own little private hell as best they knew how. All of the training exercises were invaluable to our chances for survival, but as mentioned earlier, they in no way can simulate the avalanche of emotions that occurs in these circumstances.

It didn't take very long before "Corpsman" and "Doc" were being called out from various locations on the hillside. I was scared to the core of my soul, but with shaky knees and an aching gut, I moved from one casualty to the next. Again I tried my level best to ignore my surroundings and focus on what had to be done. Above all, I had to convey to the marine I was attending to that I was confident and in control, and that he would be all right. My job wasn't to kill the enemy. That was theirs to do. I never worried about our men not getting the most out of themselves and their equipment. My job was to remain steady, at least in my own mind, and to emphasize to each of my patients that they were going to be okay. I asked them to take it easy and calm down while we got things fixed up together. If one of a marine's wounds was so severe that I didn't think that things were going to be okay, I still carried on in a positive but serious manner in my dialogue with him. Most of them knew their situation, but it was still very important for them to not perceive a negative or dire reaction from me in any way, shape, or form. It was critical to not let those who were wounded go into shock or hysteria, and I know to this day that talking to them and, above all else, reassuring them was as important as the medical treatment they received. To that point, most of the casualties that I treated had suffered gunshot wounds. Some were not as serious as others in terms of where on their body the injury had occurred. Bullets were not discriminatory. They found their way into and sometimes out of the arms, legs, and trunk area of these young men.

I was "Doc" to the guys in my unit and to everyone I met in my normal work routine. This was my handle in our daily conversations or if they needed something. For example, "Hey, Doc, can you take a look at my ankle?" I don't believe that I ever let them know it verbally, but I was honored by this and felt the obligation that went along with their trust in me. When they needed me like they did on this day, it was "Corpsman" that they cried out, which was tantamount with "Urgent! Needed now!" As fearful as I was, I always felt the pressure to get to my patient as fast as possible. It was difficult for me to occasionally make them wait because I was still attending to one of their buddies. More importantly, I had no idea as to the extent of their wounds, which made any delays even worse, at least in my mind. There would be no waiting for someone to bring the patient to where I was. That was not going to happen.

We advanced up the hill as the battle continued into the day, then *wham*, a loud explosion went off directly behind but slightly downhill from where I was. In an instant the familiar smell of gunpowder, the sight of dust and dirt everywhere, and the slight pause before the calls for help penetrated the air simultaneously dominated the scene. In addition to small-arms fire, we now were receiving incoming mortar fire, which looked to be deadly accurate and was scattered all about the hillside. Unless they had taken part in the Korean conflict or World War II, I was sure that the vast majority of our unit had never experienced anything remotely like this.

Down the hill, not very far away, was a young marine who had taken much more of the impact from the mortar round explosion than the other casualties, including myself. His entire arm was mangled, in addition to some other serious wounds, all of which required immediate attention. It took me some time to dress his wounds and stabilize him under these conditions. We were in the open area, and there was no brush and not much cover anywhere on this barren-assed hillside where we could hide. Bullets were whizzing overhead, and I had the feeling that we were out in the open and exposed way too much for our own good. I worked as rapidly as I could before Charlie could zero in on us. I had no idea whether they could actually aim in on us, but my primary objective was to get the marine moved as soon as possible to a more secure spot.

I remember feeling hatred for those who had done this to him. All that I really wanted to do was to put him back the way he was, as if this had not happened. He was a nice, quiet guy from somewhere down South, as I remember from seeing him around, and he probably wasn't yet twenty-one years old. He never complained or cried out in his pain all the while I was treating him. I affixed a medical tag to his shirt with all the information written on it for the next group of medical personnel who would treat him. In his case, he received morphine for his pain, which was only used on a case-by-case basis. It also meant he had a large letter "M" marked on his forehead for all to see that he had received this medication. Even in the midst of such chaos, we couldn't skip over any of the details from our training.

To say it was hard to concentrate only on the needs of my patients is an understatement. My primary function was to take care of their medical needs, but for my own sake I had to at least be aware of my surroundings since I was in the line of fire as much as anyone else. The Viet Cong had no qualms about shooting medical personnel, noncombatant or not. I also had to use my common sense, which meant that I couldn't run off to the next patient without moving my current one to a secure area, and to someone's else's attention. I couldn't merely yank a marine away from his primary job or jeopardize what he was doing, but no one ever declined my request for help in transporting a casualty. Sometimes they didn't know what to do or when to do it, so it was not difficult to enlist some help when we needed to move a patient to safety. All I had to do was to take charge and act like I had done this many times before, which unfortunately did become true as the day passed. If I had waited for someone else to do something, the patient would not have been moved.

Occasionally I was fortunate enough to have a couple of designated litter bearers close by who could transport the patient. As I mentioned, the poncho was the litter of choice, but it was not the easiest to grip, lift, and run with in a coordinated and smooth manner. We made every attempt to transport those who were wounded without reinjuring them, but it was not an easy task considering the wide array of circumstances. For example, some guys' strides were bigger than others, the ground was very often uneven and rocky, and four men attempting to perform a vital function in a harmonized manner while enemy forces were trying to kill us were all challenges to overcome as we moved our patients to safer ground.

As I've also said, I couldn't afford through my own actions, expressions, or body language to cause additional panic in someone who was wounded. It wasn't possible to ignore the sounds of the rounds snapping and whizzing overhead or occasionally hitting the dirt close by, but if I had dared to focus on those things, I wouldn't have been able to function. The exploding mortar rounds were intimidating, and I was more worried about them than about getting shot. I confess that it helped me psychologically to keep moving as I shifted from patient to patient. I'd always heard that a moving target was harder to hit than a stationary one anyway. I didn't do this out of bravery, but the compelling need for me to get to the next patient enabled me to move around to where I was needed the most. Whatever situation my company personnel found themselves in automatically compelled me to action. . . . They needed help, and that was all that it took to keep me going. I have seen statistics indicating that the number of medical personnel killed during the Vietnam War was disproportionally high when compared with other military actions (one-half the number killed during WWII). I make no assumptions about why this was, but I don't believe that the enemy personnel in WWII or Korea were any more or less honorable about shooting medical noncombatant personnel than those we fought in Vietnam.

I don't remember how long we were navigating these hills, but it was later in the afternoon that all of us had reached the high ground. All the while during our ascent we engaged in firefights with an enemy force who didn't appear to be going anywhere soon. The details of how many people I gave medical assistance to escapes my memory, but I do remember that among my patients was a photojournalist who needed treatment. He had sustained a shrapnel injury that was not life-threatening, but it no doubt hurt, because he was yelling like hell in any case. He was the same person who captured the photographs on the previous pages. I also caught from that first mortar shell earlier in the day a small metal fragment that became embedded in my upper left arm. It was very small, but it bled a small amount. Someone witnessed it and remembered it or wrote it down for the record, as I would later learn.

I was near exhaustion like everyone else as we pushed over the top of the largest hill. I read somewhere that the water requirement for someone on this type of military operation was two gallons per day. I can attest that we were about a gallon and a half short of that amount. The enemy fire had receded considerably for the time being, and our casualties were being airlifted out. The scene was beyond chaotic with all of the noise, dirt blowing around, the need to ensure the most seriously wounded were evacuated first, and the threat of enemy fire. By now some of our company personnel had pushed farther ahead, setting up a protective perimeter. All of my corpsmen had a more than busy day, and they all did highly commendable work under extreme circumstances.

Later in the day I learned that one of my corpsmen had been killed. He was my friend from back in Hawaii, and I was devastated by this news. His platoon, which was to be near the headquarters section in the center of our three platoons, ended up to the right side of our line of progression. Since I was one corpsman short, I had planned it so that he and I would cover the middle, and the other two platoons would have two corpsmen each to even out the manpower. In the chaos and action early on, their platoon had been repositioned to our right likely out of the response necessary at the time to counter the enemy fire. The marines who cared for my friend told me that he was mortally wounded, did not suffer, and that he did receive proper care. This man was the same corpsman whom I discussed earlier as having shot a Viet Cong guerrilla while on patrol.

That I was more than a little numb from what had just happened was probably a good thing. Otherwise I may have broken down right then and there. Once again, I had to accept the finality of the circumstances, because there was no going back for a do-over. I couldn't go for a walk to escape the moment or talk with someone about how I was feeling. If I needed a reminder, all I had to do was look down at my clothes and see the bloodstains from all those in more trouble than I. I couldn't scream out at the top of my lungs about how fucking stupid this whole exercise was. Somehow I was able to push off my eventual emotional reaction to this news until the dark of night when I would reflect in private on the horrors of the day. Then I could have my private tears for him, and for all who died and those who were hurting. I looked for his name on the Vietnam Memorial Wall when I have had the opportunity to view it.

We advanced a few more kilometers after we topped the hill and had evacuated the remaining casualties by helicopter. At this point we only encountered small pockets of enemy resistance. Most of us were just going through the motions now anyway. Reports were coming in from some of our sister companies in the battalion. They also had experienced solid enemy resistance and had suffered casualties. One of them, Hotel Company, had sustained worse casualties than we did, and the others, thankfully, were more fortunate in this regard than we were. I later read that Company H apparently landed right in the middle of a large Viet Cong unit that not only vastly outnumbered them but were known to be excellent fighters. I knew some of the corpsmen who were with Hotel Company, and my imagination was running wild thinking about what they were encountering. We were too far away from them to be of assistance. It was good to stop for the night and just roll up on the ground. I felt like I had been in a fistfight with two guys at the same time, but at least I was alive. I wondered, *How could people hate each other enough to do this to one another?* I'm glad I was a corpsman caring for others, because I actually believe that being in this situation blocked my worrying about my own mortality.

My mind was swirling around the day's events and images. I remember the first sergeant from our company walking around during all of the action, barking out orders to his men, and it appeared as if he were taking notes like a football coach who was watching over his team. He seemed oblivious to his surroundings, and he never suffered a scratch that I saw. Mostly though, within the darkness of the night all I remember feeling was an incredible sense of loss in addition to almost complete physical exhaustion. At least I got some sleep. I really didn't want much quiet time to think about stuff anyway. Thank God I wasn't a marine who had to pull guard duty that night like normal, even after all that he had gone through on this day. That is how it was: no excuses.

The next morning we moved on through a flatter terrain with low-lying hills surrounding us. There was small-arms fire coming from in front of us and off to our sides from time to time. Every time this occurred I waited for the intensity to build like it did the day before, but it did not. We steadily moved on toward the coastline, but there were no mortars or sustained firefights. I think that the Viet Cong may have had enough from the day before, and as a result they were pulling back. I didn't realize it then, but there were other large military units pushing in from all directions closing in on Charlie just as planned by those in command. I read later that there were some five thousand of us involved in this operation—naval forces, air support, and other marine contingents all working together to eliminate the threat to the Chu Lai airbase. Late in the afternoon we reached the end point of our part in the operation. Prisoners were being gathered together for transport, and other activities were ongoing as we prepared for the night. It was as pleasant as it could be under the circumstances, standing there on the peninsula looking out from the cliffs to the beautiful sea below.

Out of nowhere the ground shook and the dirt around us erupted in successions of microbursts, as if the earth itself was boiling. We were being strafed and fired upon by a couple of our own naval jet aircraft. Everyone hugged the ground, but there was no place to go or hide. It was over as fast as it started, with the battalion commander, Lieutenant Colonel "Bull" Fisher, yelling into the radio in a very clear and profane manner for them to cease fire. I don't remember anyone getting hit by these rounds, but it was definitely an unforgettable event for which I'm sure someone higher up the chain of command received an ass-chewing supreme. Most of us were still in a quasi–state of shock from the day before, and it was beginning to sink in that some of our guys were not with us any longer. Realization also set in that we were lucky to be alive, and that hopefully this military operation was helpful in the bigger scheme of things. After hand-washing my clothing back at base camp, the bloodstains on my uniform were eventually reduced to darkened blemishes, but they were no more removed from my clothes than were the memories that had been seared into my mind. In fact, those stains were constant reminders of the sacrifices some good people made for the success of the mission. I knew one thing for sure, and that was that we all got a closer look of what hell must be like during day one of the operation.

It was reported back to us that Operation Starlite was a military success, and that some four hundred to five hundred Viet Cong had been killed along with a sizeable number of prisoners captured. Dependent on the source, some news accounts had it as high as six hundred enemy combatants killed, with our casualties listed as fifty to sixty marines and one hospital corpsman killed. According to my own estimates, which were borne out later, there were on the order of four people wounded for every one who was killed in action.

As I indicated, *LIFE* magazine published a feature story about the operation, as did some other civilian and military publications. There may have been something on television, too, but I don't remember hearing anything about that. Television coverage of the war became a routine evening news event later on. We didn't have the luxury of sitting around and fretting over what might have been. There wasn't time for that, and there was always something more to do. The primary objective was to survive and go home, hopefully in the same basic condition that we came over here in, but no one ever forgot about those who didn't.

Over the next few months we carried out routine patrols and operations in the immediate area as well as at times when we traveled by chopper to farther-away destinations. We were still housed in large tents with cots to sleep on, and hot chow was available, at least some of the time. This was a far cry from the hilltops we lived on the first few months in Vietnam. We didn't get too comfortable, which was a good thing, because later there would be other hills to live on as the war expanded, along with the size of the American presence. Even though we were in a more secure setting, I still had my .45-caliber pistol loaded, including a round in the chamber, safety on, and lying within arm's length every night. I was determined that both my weapon and I would be 100 percent ready if we were ever attacked during the hours we were supposed to be sleeping.

Even though it was a much smaller mission than Operation Starlite, another event that sticks in my mind included a lengthy hike into a densely forested area. If I recall correctly, we may have ridden part of the way in troop transport trucks with machine guns mounted on swivel-type turrets over the cabs. This type of transportation was not a common occurrence and was kind of nice for a change. After walking for some time, we stopped for the night, and I remember the constant sounds of artillery rounds gliding directly over us and then exploding at what sounded like only a short distance up ahead. The word was that these rounds were being fired from naval ships offshore and were being used to soften up enemy forces in the area. My thought was that those forces must be sizeable due to all the heavy shelling. I don't remember ever having this type of support while on patrol, at least not in advance of engaging the enemy.

We had stopped, and I was just getting comfortable making friends with some C-Rations when a loud explosion echoed through the woods not a great distance away. It was pitch-black that night, and all I heard was a commotion and the screams of a young marine who had been severely wounded by what most everyone, including myself, thought to be a short round. To avoid making a target out of ourselves, we had to be very careful with the use of any light sources. All we had were a couple of flashlights with some guys standing around us as a light shield. After cutting his pant leg away, I determined that he had arterial bleeding within his upper leg in addition to having severe damage to the leg itself.

I controlled the bleeding by immediately applying a tourniquet firmly to his leg and secured pressure dressings to the other injuries he suffered.

Tourniquets were always applied with caution because of the danger of causing greater damage to the patient, but in this case there was no other choice and certainly no time to do anything else. Even though I could barely see, I know it worked because I saw the blood stop pumping out of the artery as soon as I tightened down the tourniquet. I may have used a hemostat (forceps) to pinch off the artery, I don't remember, but I know that the weeds and dirt, coupled with the darkness, the patient's mental state, and the seriousness of his wounds, made for one hell of a work environment. At least no one was shooting at us. These treatments along with some morphine for pain injected into his thigh at least made it possible for him to hold on until we could evacuate him. I don't remember how we did the med-evacuation in this forested area, but I know we got him out of there as quickly as possible and back to the battalion aid station or another facility where the staff could attend to him.

For the rest of the night, the shells whistled overhead, but no more short rounds came in—or whatever the cause was for this happening, such as a targeting error, for example. They didn't sound like typical artillery rounds, so maybe they actually were from way out on the sea. It didn't make any difference, for I had little trust that they would all make it over our asses the rest of the night. A normal person would probably be a little scared in this situation, but I became pissed—pissed that once again we had to accept getting shafted by friendly fire. There were no other disasters that night. The next day we advanced deeper into the wooded area, but we didn't encounter any sustained enemy resistance. They no doubt knew early on that we were there, and with all the noise we made the previous night they likely left in a hurry. I don't think any of us would ever know for sure. Maybe the big guns drove them out. Sometimes it seemed that we engaged the Viet Cong when we least expected it, and when we were geared up for a larger encounter, nothing much would happen. This situation was much too complicated for this corpsman to figure out. I had plenty to do without worrying about enemy strength, their movements, or even our own tactics.

I think the reason this particular military operation sticks in my mind is that it paints a representative picture as another example of what the horror of war looks like without the enemy even being involved. In a dark and foreboding night exercise in an area far from the base camp, large guns are firing a steady volley of rounds over our heads to an enemy we are looking for in the dark. Even the area up ahead didn't appear that inviting at first glance. What is not supposed to happen does occur, though, and a round from one of the large guns explodes inside our encampment area. A young marine is horribly wounded, conditions for treating him are terrible, and we wait all night long for the other shoe to drop— all while waiting for the enemy to emerge from the shadows. At least that would have been understandable. I know which event I was more afraid of, and it didn't involve Charlie directly.

NINE

A Rose for Your Nose, Doc: Merry Christmas to All

Sometime in October, while I was attending to my business and bothering no one, our company gunnery sergeant came over to where I was. "Doc, go get a clean uniform on. You're goin' to get a rose pinned on your nose this morning." I had no idea what in the hell he meant, but he didn't act mad at me, which was a good thing. He could be kind of weird in a good-natured way, so I put on the best clean clothes I had and boarded a jeep that was taking me somewhere, but I wasn't sure where or what for. . . . Talk about weird. I soon found out that a couple of guys whom I didn't know and myself were being transported to an airstrip not far away. When we arrived at the airstrip there were a dozen or more guys milling around waiting for someone to tell us supposedly why we were here. I believe that the other men were from other units in the area. I didn't recognize anyone from our company being there.

After a short time they had us line up in formation and informed us that General William C. Westmoreland, commander of all US forces, was flying in to present us with awards for meritorious service. I was impressed that he was making time to personally do this. Soon, a small plane circled in for a landing, and the general and his aides walked over to where we were. One by one, he came down the line. "Where you from, son?" When he came to me he asked me where I was from. I said, "Hooper, Nebraska." He said, "What's that?" like almost everyone else who has asked me that question. He then presented me with a Bronze Star Medal with Combat V for valor, and I cannot remember whether he also presented me with my Purple Heart, although I believe that I received it later, for the small shrapnel wound to my arm. He looked me square in the eye and said, "Good job!" before moving on down the line to the next person.

I was shocked, to put it mildly, since I had no idea this was going to occur. The general wasn't intimidating, and in fact I think that he set us at ease by his evenhanded demeanor. He didn't need to act brash or anything as he had four stars on his collar, which said it all. There were others in my Company who I felt should have been standing here also, or maybe even instead of me, which made for a mixed bag emotionally. A lengthy citation describing the actions I was involved in during Operation Starlite accompanied my Bronze Star. The citation, which is a highly generous depiction of my activities, is shown in Figure 9.1. The military was to have sent me a permanent citation, but I do not remember ever receiving it. I also don't remember ever requesting it. This one is enough.

I never did learn who recommended me for such an award, but I always suspected it was the first sergeant who was taking all the notes and moving around so much during that first day in the hills. He would never reveal that it was him, and it wasn't something one asked about. To be so honored by the Marine Corps was humbling then, and still is to this day. When I received the Purple Heart, I decided at that moment that if I ever sustained another wound like the one in my arm, it would be known to me alone. The patients I treated during Operation Starlite deserved their Purple Heart medals much more than I did.

After the brief yet organized awards ceremony, General Westmoreland returned to his plane and flew off to carry on with his many duties. He did have a war to run, after all. The rest of us rode back to our units. I didn't know what to expect from the marines and my fellow corpsmen when I got back. I wasn't worried about it overall, but I definitely wondered what everyone would think about this. Normally, I was a quiet but sociable guy, and I wasn't comfortable attracting this much attention to myself, let alone receiving accolades such as these for what I considered to be my job. What the hell else was I supposed to do that day?

Everyone wanted to see the medal, which was fastened in a simple but respectfully decorated blue storage case along with its companion ribbon. A lot of the guys congratulated me on the award, and of course there were some good-natured barbs about heroes and such tossed my way over the next couple of days. I put the medal in my permanent storage bag, but word got around about it. I remember from this time forward in my tour of duty a quiet sense of admiration from the men. I was embarrassed but proud at the same time for the recognition, but I sure wasn't about to lose perspective. Now I knew what the gunny meant by pinning a rose on my nose, that ornery old fart. When I told my parents and others back home, they were proud, too, but all they wanted to know was that I was okay. The next couple of months were generally quiet, with no major operations on the horizon, but then again we wouldn't be receiving much of a warning if there had been.

Small squad-sized ambushes were set up at night, but patrols were more often carried out during the day. One exception to this practice involved a brief but intense firefight during a night patrol adjacent to a small river. The red tracer rounds—specific rounds that are illuminated at precise intervals during bursts of fire from automatic weapons, such as machine guns—were tracking back and forth across the river like hundreds of fireflies. This way, the gunner could better locate where his firepower was directed.

"Doc, help, I've been shot!" shouted a young marine somewhere up ahead of me in the darkness.

"Where are you hit?" I answered back while trying to identify his position and keep myself low to the ground, along with everyone else.

"In the neck," he said, which meant I had to get to him now. All at once everyone was yelling, "Cease fire, cease fire," and the firing of rounds from across the river had also stopped. It seems that we were in about a one-minute engagement with some marines from another unit who were not known to be in this area, and obviously they didn't know about us either. I made it to my patient, who had luckily only been grazed by a bullet and suffered no serious injury. Thank God no one else was hurt either. I was just glad that it was stopped before things truly became more deadly. I am sure that some animated postaction discussions were carried out behind the scenes by those in charge. Hopefully, everyone learned from this experience.

Since we moved from the big hill it seemed that the patrols included more personnel and covered more distance. It was not unusual to involve a platoon or two, have a chopper ride, and spend one or two nights away from base camp. On one such patrol we were in dense jungle-type terrain, and everyone was tired and wet after being harassed by sporadic enemy fire during the day. We came upon these barn-sized holes in the ground, which created a bizarre scene the likes of which none of us had witnessed. We were informed that these craters were from two-thousand-pound bombs likely dropped by our B-52s. I know that I felt very small and somewhat uneasy thinking about the destructive power it took to create these holes. It was eerily quiet, which made me feel even more like we were treading in a space where we didn't belong.

We were moving along in single file, maneuvering around the edge of one of these craters, when one of our guys fell down its side and into the hole, badly injuring one of his ankles. I stabilized his ankle and gave him something for the pain. It took us a while to get him out of the hole. He was embarrassed. A couple of the guys were less than sympathetic in some of their remarks. I think they felt sorry for him but also viewed this as a careless accident. Nevertheless, after carrying him for a time he had to be evacuated out by chopper when it could be arranged. I'm sure that this created more of a ruckus than the company commander had wanted. Who knows, maybe he wanted them to know we were in the area. We definitely spent considerable time and effort on these search-and-destroy missions to find and engage the insurgents. The timing for engagement wasn't up to us alone, that much was certain. But at least they knew we were in the area. Even though we had only the occasional sniper fire, I was more than willing to return to familiar surroundings. Maybe my imagination was working overtime, but this area had an ominous and particularly remote atmosphere.

We were becoming more and more hardened as our tour of duty progressed. We were involuntarily in the process of wearing away any remnants of innocence we had brought with us to this hellhole. As Christmas approached, I remember us being temporarily deployed near the ever expanding and well-used Chu Lai airstrip along the beach. We had cots to sleep on inside large canvas-covered structures with actual wooden floors in them. There was considerable work activity in the area, and many more people around than I was accustomed to. There were also

UNITED STATES MARINE CORPS
HEADQUARTERS, FLEET MARINE FORCE, PACIFIC
FPO, SAN FRANCISCO, 96601

In the name of the President of the United States, the Commanding General, Fleet Marine Force, Pacific takes pleasure in presenting the BRONZE STAR MEDAL to

HOSPITALMAN THIRD CLASS RICHARD W. SCHAEFER

UNITED STATES NAVY

for service as set forth in the following

CITATION:

"For heroic service in connection with operations involving conflict with an opposing foreign force while serving as a Company Chief Corpsman with Company E, 2d Battalion, 4th Marines in the Republic of Vietnam on 18 August 1965. After the company had taken its first objective, a low hill mass, they were beseiged by intense enemy mortar and automatic weapons fire from approximately 200 meters away on an adjacent ridge. Although wounded in the arm by fragments from the initial mortar fire, Hospitalman Third Class SCHAEFER, with complete disregard for his own wound and personal safety, fearlessly exposed himself to enemy fire in order to render aid and treatment to nearly a dozen of the fifteen wounded Marines. He further assisted and directed the evacuation of the wounded to a defiladed area, secure from small arms fire. Through his aggressiveness and coolness under fire, he undoubtedly saved the lives of several of his comrades. Hospitalman Third Class SCHAEFER's initiative and courageous actions were in keeping with the highest traditions of the United States Naval Service."

Hospitalman Third Class SCHAEFER is authorized to wear the Combat "V".

FOR THE PRESIDENT,

V. H. KRULAK
LIEUTENANT GENERAL, U. S. MARINE CORPS
COMMANDING

TEMPORARY CITATION

9.1 Citation for Bronze Star Medal with Combat "V" pertaining to Operation Starlite on August 18, 1965. Courtesy of United States Marine Corps.

some signs of military structure and protocol. No one was saluting or shining their boots, but it was obvious who had been out in the field and who had been back here more or less in the rear. The latter had cleaner clothes, better haircuts, their boots were in better shape, and they physically looked cleaner than we did. It took us a while to get that ground-in, sunbaked-dirt look after all. We wore it with a certain sense of pride.

I don't think I realized until then how independent and in some ways rebellious we grunts had become. No one in the field was going to hold

9.2 A celebration among the men of the battalion aid station. Courtesy of H. Krentel, fellow hospital corpsman

9.3 Fellow hospital corpsmen and I (far left), possibly Christmas 1965. Courtesy of H. Krentel, fellow hospital corpsman

our hand and bark orders at us regarding the small stuff. No one was going to do our thinking for us. Survival and destroying the enemy forces were the priorities, and the more we were out in the field where the action was, the more this was reinforced on a daily basis. Insignia indicating military rank was not worn in the field for the purpose of not identifying to the enemy who was who. We didn't need to display our rank, because we all knew each other, who was in charge, and who did which job. One quick way to get knocked on your rear was to salute an officer in the field, thus identifying him for the enemy to snipe at.

During this little Christmas break, I had the opportunity to meet up with some of my corpsmen buddies from battalion, making it a reunion of sorts. Being out in the field most of the time, I hadn't seen many of them that much since Okinawa, and the timing of this break around the holidays was a welcome respite, if only for a few days. I remember this Christmas for singing carols, drinking beer, playing cards, and simply shooting the bull about old times. Mostly, we all read and reread our mail from home and thought of what we were missing out on, each in our own unique way. We also consumed lots of chocolate chip cookies, because my mother shipped me boxes of them routinely. Their shelf life was very short due to the humidity and heat, which was a good excuse for devouring them in no time at all.

While I was stationed in Hawaii, I was away from home at Christmas, so this was not a new experience for me, just one that sucked, especially when someone played "I'll Be Home for Christmas." There would always be next year. It was really good not to have to sleep with my pistol directly at my side, but I also didn't want to get used to this as a frame of reference. I didn't overanalyze it, but I knew even at my young age that I had to maintain whatever my edge consisted of, so that I could stay sharp enough to make it back home. It was probably a good thing to stay tightly wound, because it wasn't long before we pulled back into the surrounding countryside where we had work to do. I probably could have requested to stay back at the battalion aid station, but there was no way I was going to leave my infantry company. Too late now.

With the advent of the New Year (1966), did I dare even think about becoming a short-timer and leaving in May? The answer was no, because it was too far off and potentially dangerous to focus on. I would keep it as a good thought for now. Sometimes those who worried too much about getting short ended up getting hurt, or so it was thought. Maybe it seemed that way because everyone felt an extra ache of sadness when someone who was close to leaving didn't make it. The best approach was to keep thinking and concentrating on one day at a time, because that is exactly how things played out.

TEN

R & R in Saigon

After a few months, a program was established that allowed for small numbers of us to leave for R & R (rest and relaxation). Some guys went to more exotic destinations such as Thailand, the Philippines, or even Hawaii for three to four days to get away from the war zone and to recharge their batteries. Everyone was supposed to get their turn, but I was never convinced that it was managed in the most efficient manner. It was never explained how this system worked regarding who went and where. In any case, my turn came up somehow, and I was assigned Saigon (present-day Ho Chi Minh City), the capital of South Vietnam, as my destination for three days. As usual, we received no advance notice, but none of us wasted any time getting down to the airfield. One of my fellow corpsmen and I, along with a contingent of marines, boarded a large cargo plane and flew south to Saigon. I didn't know what to expect, but I envisioned hot showers, clean sheets, hot meals, and pretty Vietnamese girls. As it turned out I had some, but not quite all, of these attributes correct.

What a huge, bustling city Saigon was: Thousands of small motor scooters, bicycles, rickshaws, buslike vans, and some automobiles blanketed the streets. Our contingent of troops along with others from various duty assignments were transported by bus to a large hotel that was under the control of our military. The other corpsman from my unit and

I shared a room. We had bunk beds, clean sheets, and cold showers, but it was a safe environment, or so it appeared. We were given some dos and don'ts, along with basic information about the area. For the most part we were cut loose during the day and evening and had to be back at the hotel by midnight.

One of the first things my corpsman buddy and I did was to have a large breakfast of fried eggs, meat, and any other American food they could shove in our faces. It had been awhile since either one of us had eaten like that. We rode a rickshaw around downtown Saigon, and I remember at one stoplight in particular, it seemed like everyone around us was staring at me, and for all I knew, they were. Even though our military and the South Vietnamese Army presence was everywhere, there still weren't many light-haired Americans wandering around the city in those days. We had planned to call home, but the way that it was set up was not optimal, and the lines waiting to make calls were way too long. Instead we took our rickshaw ride out to a large military store just to check it out and be in a more familiar and comfortable setting. I think we basically wanted to be around some Americans doing normal things. We did manage some time for sightseeing, but we didn't stray too far from the area we knew visually. With all the Vietnamese people around us at any given time, if something would have happened to us, they wouldn't have easily found us.

The city was very alive and architecturally beautiful in its own right, along with the hustle and bustle of all the activity on the streets and sidewalks. Possibly it was due to the fact that we were in a city within a war-torn country, but it was difficult to view it any differently. The adult people dressed much better than those in the rural areas, but they did not appear to be overtly affluent. There were masses of poor people, many of them children, all along the sidewalks and even crowding out onto the streets on the busier corners. They were trying to make a living any way they could. Scores of panhandlers were everywhere, but we were aware of what could happen if we had decided to hand them money. It was difficult to ignore them, but we dared not get involved in their business. Everyone gave the impression of having somewhere to go, and to this small-town guy it appeared as if they were all headed for the same place at the same time.

Even though everyone seemed friendly enough, we decided that we needed to get off of the street. We stood out too much to ever be comfortable, especially at night. We came across a friendly little drinking establishment with some pretty bar girls who would sit with anyone responding to their request, "You buy for me some Saigon tea?" There were numerous wild and more exotic bars along the street, but neither my friend nor I were experienced party boys. We didn't want to get involved in anything too far over our heads. The concept, at least in the bar we came to frequent, was that we would spend money for drinks and for every drink we bought, we also purchased one for the person we were sitting with. It was not a huge price to pay for a little female companionship in order to learn more about the Asian ways or the Vietnamese culture. In other words we just wanted someone to be with besides other military guys.

Some of these girls were noticeably good looking, while others were made up to look beautiful. I soon formed a rapport with one young lady who was very nice and quite good looking. My fellow corpsman and I sampled every beer known to be sold in Vietnam, or so it seemed, but neither of us got to the point where we couldn't defend ourselves, or at least run like hell, should the need arise. We also made it back to our hotel on time each night, but never did we feel safe to the point of letting our guard down, as stated earlier. Spending this R & R time in Saigon was not the same as if we were in the Philippines, no matter how hard we tried to ignore the fact that we were still in Vietnam.

One afternoon my buddy and I decided to ask our newfound friends to go see a movie matinee with us. I don't think they knew what to think, but they viewed it as a treat and accepted our invitation. Since they were bar girls they were required to walk ahead of us, not with us, as we walked together to the theater. I don't think they could be seen with us in public because of their occupation as bar girls or their culture, I'm not sure. Hell, maybe they were members of the Viet Cong, but I don't think that was the case at all. The theater was a huge and very ornate building. The movie, which had subscripts, was mildly entertaining, and we had the whole place to ourselves. The girls seemed to enjoy being with us, watching the movie, and getting out of the bar, too. They weren't making much money for the bar while at the movie, but no one seemed to mind. How many guys can say they went to a movie in Saigon on a weekday afternoon?

Overall, we had a good time on our R & R break, spending too much money in the bar, but I guess I'll always believe that all the girls who operated the bar genuinely liked us. We did nothing to disrespect them or their country while we were there, and we didn't lose our heads in the bottom of the beer bottles. I made a feeble attempt at propositioning the young woman I spent most of my time with, but she said she had commitments to someone up north who was fighting in the war. *Probably an enemy insurgent*, I thought to myself. Instead, she offered me to go along with her sister for a private little encounter away from the bar. Even though I was disappointed that it wouldn't be with her, it was something to ponder, and I didn't want to disrespect her or her sister. The outcome of this decision is no doubt of interest only to me.

When it came time for our last day in their city, we thanked all the gals in our little getaway for their hospitality and friendship. By the time we had left there, I don't think we had to pay for every beer we consumed like the other customers did, and we took away a few memories from South Vietnam that didn't include death and destruction. I would have liked to have gone to Bangkok to see what it was like there, but as it turned out I am glad that I saw more of Vietnam. It was time to head back many miles to the north, to get back to doing what we were in Vietnam for in the first place, which was our jobs, not to sit in a bar while others worked. For some reason, though, I didn't feel that guilty for the three days away. I did feel guilty that I didn't find a way to call home.

Once we were back in the field, it didn't take very long to get back in the groove. There were forays when we expelled a considerable amount of effort and got very little out of it as a result. One such operation comes to mind, not for the violence or excitement that occurred, but more for the uniqueness of the experience. It was a large undertaking, with us launching by helicopter toward what I would label as mountainous terrain. It was a long trip, and I don't think we had ever flown before at that high of an altitude or as far inland.

We were far away from the usual grassy pastures and rice paddies as the choppers dropped us off onto the side of a mountain. I wasn't exactly sure what our mission was, but from where we were positioned I could see for miles in most any direction. Off in the distance in between and high over the mountains, huge helicopters airlifted artillery and other heavy equipment to points unknown. These large choppers may have been US Army, I'm not sure, but we had not observed such a large movement of equipment since being in South Vietnam. It was an impressive undertaking. I felt as though we were looking at the continued buildup of our power base, which would indicate a protracted commitment to this country.

Likely we were there for intelligence gathering or for security as part of some larger objective. We patrolled out into the heavily wooded, junglelike environment. The topography was beautiful, with a dense canopy overhead and thick vegetation everywhere we went. I was looking for but didn't see any wild animals, which was true during my entire tour of duty in Vietnam. We used to joke around that the Vietnamese probably ate them, since they were thought to be ingenious at making a little rice and a small amount of meat last a long time. Actually, it was no joking matter. The Viet Cong traveled very lightly in comparison to us, partly because they could extend their rations out very effectively. Unfortunately, this only helped them be better combatants than they already were. I carried two canteens, a .45-caliber pistol, a large knife, and battle dressing all fastened to my large webbed belt. I also had a medical bag, helmet, backpack, poncho, extra socks, food, a shovel, and sometimes a flak jacket.

During this operation I had the impression that we were expecting some heavy resistance at any time, but it just didn't come. We saw no people. I think this operation may have taken us farther away from Chu Lai than we had been, or it may have only seemed this way because of the remoteness of the area. Not only were we higher up in mountainous terrain, but we also were in jungles very similar to those in Hawaii. Moving through this type of landscape made for the ominous feeling that we could be attacked at any time due to the limited visibility, along with the feeling of being isolated. After a few days perched in the mountains and tromping through the rain and the slick trails of the jungle, we moved out and flew back to Chu Lai, which looked good to us. This was one of the few times we didn't at least get shot at by Charlie. It was a lot of work for no real measure of success in terms of destroying the enemy. At least

I could see firsthand the topographical diversity of this faraway land. Seeing such unique geographical areas almost dampened the torment of being engaged in a full-time war effort, if only for a very short time.

The longer we were in Vietnam, the more frequently we encountered some form of enemy resistance on our patrols. It could have been that we were out on more patrols, or that some of us were getting nearer to going home and were imagining this to be true; however, I think it may have been that our intelligence-gathering ability had improved regarding enemy locations. If ammunitions, weapons, maps, or any other enemy contraband were found in a village, it was taken or destroyed. Houses and structures were burned to the ground, which in some ways felt contrary to our mission of helping the people of this country. Enemy sanctuary or even the potential of such a safe haven had to be eliminated for our own protection. The Viet Cong had enough strongholds already in place. Even though I understood all of that, there was a subtle uneasiness for me in seeing their homes burned to the ground as they looked on. I don't think I was the only one who felt that way.

The more often we engaged the enemy and took even light casualties, the more it wore on us. On some level we were becoming more warlike and callous in our behavior. Everyone was getting better and better at their jobs from a physical vantage point, but psychologically, it appeared to me that some of the stress points were being stretched thin. It wasn't only the emotional drain of engaging the enemy, but the more cumulative impact of having to be ready at all times, and not knowing when or if confrontation was close at hand. Even without any contact with Charlie, the day-in, day-out, relentless heat, lousy food, hot water to drink, sore feet kicking up dust on more meaningless trails, and constant sweat drenching our clothes had a way of affecting even the most positive attitudes. These were the days when placing one foot in front of the other seemed to be enough. In a twisted way it was almost better to engage with the enemy than to experience the sheer boredom of walking endlessly around the landscape. That is, of course, until we actually met up with him.

ELEVEN

Standing in Hell's Doorway

As we had done so many times before, we all boarded helicopters one morning and took a brief chopper ride to what appeared to be a serene pastureland commingled with a sea of rice paddies. In fact, the sizeable village we were approaching had many of these paddies surrounding it. I don't remember anyone talking up this operation as anything that noteworthy, but I do recollect that we had solid information that this particular village, which was in the Quang Ngai region, was under the control of the Viet Cong. It was a fairly large and spread-out circular-shaped compound with tall palm trees within its borders and rice fields surrounding its perimeter. The rice paddies were almost moat-like from a functional perspective, as they physically defended the interior of the village itself. The land was very flat, with no hills and few trees out in the open areas, not significantly different in general appearance from the valley back in Nebraska where my family lived.

We were dropped off a safe distance from the village where we got everyone organized, formed up, and prepared to launch an assault. Echo Company platoons were to my right and left, which presented a formidable presence for whatever lay ahead. Up to this point there was no resistance, and we took no action. We spread out and began our advance toward the rice paddy area some distance away. It was mid-March 1966, and as usual, it was hot as hell. At least it wasn't raining, and it wasn't dark, but it sure was quiet, with no perceivable sounds coming from the village confines—just a few puffs of smoke, likely from their cooking fires.

As we approached the large configuration of rice paddies positioned directly adjacent to the village, the familiar sound of *pop, pop, pop!* from small-arms fire ripped through the air from various locations to our front and sides. As was the case many times before, it began with sporadic bursts of firepower that was returned by our guys many times over. At this point in time, no mortar rounds were incoming, but very suddenly, enemy fire was coming at us from all along the village perimeter. We were close in near the village by now, receiving semiautomatic and fully automatic fire, including the intermittent, staccatolike sounds of larger-caliber weaponry being directed at us. All of this was punctuated with frequent explosions and had mushroomed into a very intense battle with those in the village.

There were multiple calls of "Corpsman, corpsman!" from ahead of me and to my sides. I hadn't heard this volume of firepower since being in Vietnam, not even on Operation Starlite. It was fierce and very quickly making an impact on us. My knees were shaky as usual, but at least I was moving, and I began treating the closest casualties. It was mass chaos and confusion, as I expected, coupled with misery and agony everywhere I went. I had been in this situation before, but not to this degree. What in the hell did we get ourselves into here? The enemy rounds were snapping and whizzing overhead with no letup, which did nothing for the confidence I needed to muster up going forward. They always say that you never hear the round that gets you, which makes sense, since it is moving faster than the speed of sound. Somehow that sage adage didn't do a thing to make me feel any more secure. I was definitely looking and waiting for a pause in the action that simply wouldn't come, like it always had before. Not having a break or any sign of a possible end to the enemy fire did more to rattle me than most anything else to this point. The increase in noise and firepower seemingly to never reach a crescendo or conversely a stopping point only fueled the anxiety.

As all of this was unfolding and the action level was gaining in strength, I came upon one of my corpsmen crouching down behind a paddy dike. He was shaking, but he wasn't responsive to anything I said or did. He wasn't wounded or physically hurt, but he wasn't coherent either. In my ignorance, my first reaction was to become irate toward him for not getting up and treating our casualties as I was directing him to do. I even threatened him in an attempt to bring him back to reality, but to no avail. He was an excellent corpsman and had been my good friend for a long time, but I needed him. They were yelling for us. He had seen a lot, and something unfortunately had snapped within him, pushing him over the edge so that he was physically not able to move. He had seen enough. Within a few seconds I realized what was happening to him. I attempted to comfort him and helped him back to where I hoped it would be safer area for him to wait until he could get out of there. This occurrence affected me nearly as much as anything else did that day. I wasn't ready to deal with such an experience, and I discovered that it impacted me about as much as any physical medical injury I witnessed. This was true, in part, because he was my friend and comrade, and since he reported to me, I felt somehow responsible on some level for his situation. I know that he was sent home, and I sure as hell hoped he received the treatment he needed. I undeniably missed having his help the rest of the day.

I cannot remember the sequence of events and all of the blur and details of what happened that day. It has been more than fifty years, but as I've said before, some events are seared in my mind. There definitely is the phenomena relating to the fog of war, but these lapses in memory are a result of something much more complex than I am able to express. One of the images burned into my mind involves a young marine who had been shot in the chest area. He was sitting up against a rice paddy dike; he was semiconscious and only slightly responsive. At this point we had advanced to within fifty meters, if that, to the edge of the village. The Viet Cong were entrenched and dug in all along its perimeter so that they could fire at us at will as we inched closer to their positions. I couldn't see them distinctly, only the periodic flashes from their weapons. I heard automatic weapons fire and what sounded like machine-gun fire from any number of areas. I pulled my patient down toward the ground, and even though I was on my knees, I bent as low to the ground as I could, quickly examining him for any exit wounds and for other injuries he may have sustained. Bullets were flying all around us, hitting the dirt on top of the paddy dike and buzzing over our heads.

No sooner had I affixed the battle dressings to his wounds than he suddenly lurched forward toward me with the whole right side of his neck exposed, and a split second later he was hit again along the side of his head. A crease from the back toward the front of his head was deep enough to penetrate his skull, once again causing him to lurch forward. Parts of him were on the front of my shirt. He was literally shot out of my arms. Were they trying to hit me directly, or were the dirty sons of bitches trying to shoot this man again and again? This nearly put me over the edge, but I laid him down and attended to his wounds to the best of my ability for the conditions we were under. There was no place for us to hide. He was unconscious and not responsive. I couldn't get a pulse or detect breathing, and other medical checks I made, including his pupils, indicated to me that he was gone. I communicated this information to a couple of marines nearby. I was being called over and over to go elsewhere, which I had to do. I was physically spent and mentally drained, and we had only been there about two hours. Adrenalin and fear kept moving me from spot to spot. This battle was much worse than Operation Starlite, and no one had even penetrated the village yet that I could tell. I was seriously beginning to doubt whether I was going to get out of there unharmed, yet I felt that I was being looked after—nothing special due to anything I was doing, just being watched over as I had been all of my life.

The situation was not improving. In fact, we were not advancing toward the village but appeared to be bogged down and stalled in the damn rice paddies. It sounded to me like things were intensifying. I'm certainly no military strategy expert, but even I could tell we were not getting the job done. I came up on one of our junior sergeants crouched down alongside a rice paddy dike. He had a wound to his upper leg by his rear. It was not a serious injury, and after calming him down I helped him back to a more secure area. He told me that our gunnery sergeant was lying up on the rice paddy dike to the left of where we just were, and close to the edge of the village. I scrambled back over to the dike, which led directly into the village. I got up on top of it, made my way forward, and found him lying there on his back, some twenty meters, if that, from the village border. I could have thrown a rock from where I was into the village. He was not moving, his helmet was full of blood, and unfortunately he had suffered a massive wound to the back of his head. I said a quick prayerful good-bye to the gunny, whom I barely had the chance to know. He had replaced that ornery old company gunnery sergeant I spoke of earlier. It was obvious that this younger sergeant was trying to lead the way into the village, for he was a marine's marine.

The surface of the dike was exploding all around me from the bullets striking the ground. I saw none of our guys to my right and only a couple to my far left, way down in the paddies, which meant the gunny and I were basically alone and isolated. There was no one to help me, and I knew that I shouldn't be in this situation. For the first time in Vietnam, I had a strong feeling that this may be it. The rounds sounded different somehow, and it was almost as if I could feel them around me, but I'm not sure if this is even possible. I wanted to go forward and choke somebody to death for all the misery I saw today, but that was not an option. I thought I had felt alone before, but never like this. The back of my neck hairs were signaling me to get the hell out of here now! I could just as easily have frozen in terror like a rabbit being stalked by a coyote. If I had really looked at my situation I probably would have, but instead I scampered back a few meters then down off the dike to where I had originated from, as fast as my legs would go.

As I was moving along the paddies, one of the guys informed me that my previous patient who had suffered the chest, neck, and head wounds was still alive, according to another corpsman. I saw that the corpsman had started an IV, but it had fallen out of his arm, possibly as a result of moving him. I reinserted it and attempted to secure it better as he was being carried back for evacuation. Actually, I think we were pulling back, but I just wasn't aware of this yet. I still didn't detect movement or signs of life. I hoped that I was wrong, and that somehow he would live. I felt bad and embarrassed that I may have made the wrong call in the field, but I felt no overwhelming shame considering the working conditions. I had made the decisions I did with the best information I had or knew at that point in time.

The firing began to recede to some degree as I made my way back to a clump of small trees and a large dirt pile where some other marines, including our first lieutenant in charge, were taking cover. This slight respite was due to the fact that we were pulling back, and there wasn't a lot of firepower coming from our side as this was happening. There wasn't a whole hell of lot of direction being given. As I was catching my breath, twenty-five to thirty meters away was a marine who was crawling along in the open rice paddy water calling for a corpsman. I ran to him only to find that he was just sick to his stomach and not wounded. I could have throttled him, but I draped his arm around my neck and over my shoulder, hung onto his wrist, and with my other arm around his waist we ran side by side, crouched over, with a hail of bullets splashing in the water to our sides and in front of our feet in addition to those whizzing by our heads until we made it to where the others were. In my mind's eye at the time I imagined us as track stars sprinting to safety with the athletic prowess of Olympians, but in reality I'm sure we looked rather clumsy with our canteens banging against our balls and my pistol flopping against my leg, trying our level best just to survive those last meters to safety. This was pretty dumb, and I remember feeling that I was really asking for it. I remember being pissed at the time that he didn't really need me, but he was appreciative. Who knows? Maybe he couldn't force himself to get up and run on his own.

The lieutenant asked me if I had seen the gunnery sergeant, so I updated him on what I had observed a few minutes earlier. He said, "Are you sure he was dead, Doc?" to which I replied, something to the effect of we could go back out there and he could see for himself if he wanted to take a look. I was still sensitive about what happened earlier that day regarding my patient with the severe head, chest, and neck wounds, and I didn't need the lieutenant—who wasn't long in country—quizzing me on what I had seen. He said, "Okay, Doc, okay," and backed off after I described to him the circumstances out on that dike. It was probably a case of my imagination being the problem more than any real inference being made. He informed us that we were pulling away.

We were pulling back and regrouping. The marines never say "retreat," but they refer to the action as "regrouping for another attempt." For all I knew, maybe we would be making another attempt at penetrating this village perimeter. I was up for it if anyone else was. I grabbed an M-14 rifle that was leaning against the dirt pile that we were hiding behind and fired a clip of rounds toward where I figured the enemy was located in their rat holes. I had never fired an M-14 in anger before, and it felt good to do this. The guys usually taped two clips together, so I flipped them around and fired twenty more rounds or whatever was left in the clip toward them once again, always hoping that I had hit at least one. "Come on, Doc, we're heading back to the rear." I wasn't ready to pull back yet. Besides, we left one person out there on the dike, and the marines never leave anyone behind. In this case it would have risked three or four more lives at a minimum to retrieve the gunny who had valiantly attempted to lead a charge into the village. If he would have had a few more marines behind him, he may have penetrated its perimeter. No one knows except those who were with him. There was no choice now but to pull back.

We fell back to near where we had landed that morning. I was near the headquarters group that had gathered by a small outbuilding of some sort when enemy mortars started exploding. "Corpsman, corpsman, over here," was heard immediately. I stood up and ran only a few steps before I very abruptly fell face down in the dirt. I picked myself up, feeling kind of stupid for my clumsiness, and ran over to where a couple of marines who had just began to dig in had taken a direct hit from one of the mortar rounds. They were both killed instantly by the mortar, which was the kick in my gut to end all kicks. It was too reminiscent of the artillery short round on the hill months earlier. I slowly walked back to where I had been, and someone said that I was one lucky guy. A mortar had exploded close behind me, knocking me face down in the dirt, but I didn't realize it. It did feel as if someone pushed me from behind so hard that I couldn't stand up, but I thought it was just me tripping over my own feet, a shoelace, or something else on the ground. I only remember that it happened in the blink of an eye.

All day long it felt like we were getting our asses kicked, and now they were dropping mortars down on us. What's more, from our position, we were too far away to do much about it. In no more than a few minutes, air support arrived and attacked the village with a vengeance. I had not seen so much airpower, so close up before, and they put an emphatic punishment on the village. This went on for a while, and then darkness fell, accompanied by silence and flickering fires from the village. These fires didn't look like cooking fires, however, but fires as a result of our airpower.

Nothing happened all night long. I kept thinking about our sergeant lying on the dike. Would the enemy do anything to him or take him? This had been the day I had hoped would never come in Vietnam, but it finally caught up with us. My hands and clothing bore witness to the day's events, and I had enough horrendous memories to last me a lifetime, but at least I had my life and limb. I always felt that I should or could have done more, but I don't know about this time. I was almost to the end of my rope. I was done for now.

After the airstrikes while it was still light, a small surveillance plane had flown over the area a few times. Someone said it was General Westmoreland. I don't know for sure if this was true, but then it didn't really matter to me at that point who was in it. I was just glad that we didn't try to go back in the village and take it, but if that had been the decision, I would have been ready to go in. That night, I dug a couple of small metal fragments out of my forearm that never came to anyone's attention. There would be no second Purple Heart. It was amazing that we could still manage to eat something after a day like this, but we all did.

Morning came, and we moved into the village. We walked in untouched, as the enemy was long gone. Our gunnery sergeant was still lying undisturbed where he had been. He respectfully came with the rest of us as we made our way into what formerly had been a Viet Cong stronghold. There were fighting holes and trench lines dug into the ground all around the village. I didn't see a lot of bodies, even though there apparently were some on the other side of the village perimeter. Someone reminded us that the Viet Cong drag their bodies out with them, although I read later that there were approximately one hundred fresh graves found within the compound and nearly two hundred enemy were confirmed as killed in action. The village itself was largely obliterated, and what was left of it was destroyed before we left. I couldn't help but wonder how it could have been such a hellhole only a few hours earlier, and now it was peaceful in the morning light as if the fighting never happened. Later, we were informed that there had been a very substantial enemy force in the village, and that the operation was a success in eliminating another one of their safe-harbor areas. In the perspective of finding what we were looking for, I guess it was a successful mission. It just didn't feel like one, the way it went down. I would much rather have overpowered them on their own turf that first day. This one would stick with us for a while. I was sure of that. We went back to our base area as the second day ended. Everybody cleaned up and readied themselves and their equipment in preparation for whatever else lay ahead. We all had to be at the ready this day like we were the day before, and we had to do it as if yesterday never happened. None of us would ever be the same again, though.

I would be remiss if I didn't at least state how impressed I was with my original captain, Jerry W. Ledin, the company commander. He came over with us from Hawaii, and I had the good fortune to be under his leadership for many months. He was a large man who wore suspenders and smoked a large-bowled, curved-stem pipe. He always had kind of a sly grin on his face even in the worst possible situations. It came off as being cool under pressure, at least in my opinion. He wore his responsibility well, and I know he had many private nights when he had to write letters to the parents and relatives of those who made sacrifices in the name of our unit. He had written a letter to my parents for my efforts during Operation Starlite, and later he even sent a letter thanking them for some cookies that my mom had sent for all of us to enjoy. I followed him and his men for many a mile over the hills and valleys of South Vietnam, and I would have followed him into the fires of hell itself, because he would have been the first one in. He was an effective leader whom I came to respect a great deal. His replacement was a good officer, but he had a ways to go to pull the same efforts out of his men that the captain did. I witnessed that on this latest battle, although I'm not sure what even the captain could have done better this time. There were simply too many well dug-in enemy combatants and too few of us to get at them effectively. I still missed the captain, though.

Nothing remarkable occurred over the next several weeks, except that our unit moved up north, closer to the city of Da Nang. Our mission—or at least our location—was changing. The Da Nang airbase was a very large, modern facility, as close to a stateside military airbase as we were going to get in Vietnam. I was expecting my new orders to head back to the States sometime in early May, so I wasn't overly anxious to engage Charlie, although a part of me wanted to get more accomplished before I left. Maybe that related to what happened at the village near Quang Ngai back in March, although I think there was more to it. We had not finished the job as I had imagined. Of course, I had no way of knowing that the war was just beginning for our combat troops.

The war wasn't won yet. The VC were still around, and the impression was that the North Vietnamese military was very much involved, even more so than before. The overall situation appeared to be escalating in intensity and scope. While we were still down at Chu Lai we did engage in smaller skirmishes where I found myself worrying more than normal about what might happen to me. I believe this was largely due to my being close to leaving, and I didn't want anything to mess it up. This attitude was not a good thing, and I sure as hell was glad that I didn't feel this way during my whole tour in Vietnam.

I had also received word that another of my friends who was a very good corpsman had been killed in action. He was a quiet person and just a nice guy to be around. It seemed like it was always the good guys, and I found it difficult to believe that this had happened to him. Maybe I was having these feelings because it was so damned unfair. This whole preoccupation of leaving Vietnam was a mixed bag of emotions that I was going to have to process. After all, the fellow corpsmen whom I worked with and the marine unit I was attached to were the same men I ate with, fought with, and cried with for the past year. Although we didn't talk about it, the feelings we had for each other created a bond that would not disappear just because we were not together physically.

We had good living quarters at the Da Nang location, and we kept partially busy by conducting routine sick calls for the marines on base. Mostly it was boring duty, and I was in no mood for listening to a lot of military barking and bullshit after a year of being in the field where the action was. By now, I was even more accustomed to everyone around me just doing their job together within the concept of what the military was supposed to be about, which was following orders and leading by example. I could see some of the marines struggling with readjusting, and I felt for them. We all had more time to think and reflect now than when we were down at Chu Lai. Through no fault of their own, those without our experiences could not comprehend what we needed, and I'm not sure we could have told them anyway. No one talked about it, but a lot of others, including myself, needed to decompress and readapt to what normal was. We were like, "Are you for real?" when someone actually tried to apply some silly-assed rule that might have concerned us a year before, but not now. We were changed men, and we couldn't do a thing about it, except let civility somehow welcome us back.

SUPPLEMENT TO CHAPTER ELEVEN

The following supplemental information is from other accounts written about Operation Texas, a name I had not recalled earlier while writing this book. Not only was this information interesting to me, but it augmented and supported the material in this chapter. These accounts also provided information about some of the strategies, planning activities, and big-picture narratives relating to the overall plan we were carrying out on the ground.

For example, our Second Battalion Fourth Marines (2/4) companies of Echo and Fox were in a backup role for Operation Texas, a large, multiforce operation including ARVN South Vietnamese troops—a military action that involved much more than the enemy village, Phuong Dinh, discussed in this chapter. As I noted, I don't remember a detailed briefing about our mission. Our new battalion commander, Lieutenant Colonel Paul X. Kelley, who later became commandant of the US Marine Corps, played an integral role in planning and executing the operation. My company, Echo Company, was to take the lead in attacking the village compound while Fox Company secured and controlled the landing zone.

I was not aware at the time, but Colonel Kelley had earlier called for an artillery bombardment of the village. Perhaps this occurred before we got there, I am not sure. It was reported that an aerial observer told the colonel that there was no movement on the village grounds. A few minutes later, this was reversed with a pilot flying over the compound radioing in that enemy forces were erupting out of the ground, hundreds of them, right at the same time we were beginning our attack. I now realize why this engagement appeared more severe than anything I had experienced.

According to these accounts, after only a few hours we were running low on ammunition and had only breached one layer of a small part of the village perimeter. The problem was that there were three more defensive perimeters of dug-in troops, and we could not penetrate their defenses. The reports state that Kelley's headquarters, which was only about fifty meters away from the village, had serious problems of its own, with fourteen marines killed or wounded. Kelley ordered us to pull back, and after we were away from the edge of the village, an intense air strike and artillery attack commenced. By their account, 1,346 rounds of artillery ammunition and 51 air strikes were directed at the village by late afternoon. I remember the air strikes vividly, but I'm not as clear on the artillery. I read that Kelley was considering going back for another attempt, but he calculated that company personnel strength was down to eighty to ninety men each, and he had no reserves. With the enemy being numerically superior and so well dug in, he decided to continue the attack by firepower instead. I am glad he made that decision. The following is a comment from Colonel Kelley a few days after the operation:

> The overriding problem in Operation Texas was one which had plagued the Marine Corps for many years: how to inflict maximum loss on a determined, well-entrenched enemy with complex defensive positions at a minimum loss to one's own forces. In the case of Phuong Dinh over 2,500 rounds of artillery and innumerable air strikes with napalm and heavy ordnance were called. The net result, however, indicated that the enemy in well-constructed bunkers, in holes with overhead cover and 20-feet deep tunnels was not appreciably hurt by our preparatory fires and had to be killed in his positions by infantry action at close quarters.

I realize that everyone involved cannot know, nor should they, all of the planning details associated with such a military operation. Technically I knew enough to perform my job along with those around me, and I didn't learn anything from what I read that changed my perception. On the other hand, I found some of the planning efforts they undertook, where we fit into the picture, and the statistics reported to be very interesting. I would never have known about the numbers of artillery and air strikes that helped us get the job done. Perhaps I didn't care back then about such things, but today I find this information very clarifying. Perhaps the Marine Corps could do a better job of having postoperation information sessions for the troops, which I believe would enhance their understanding and make them feel more appreciated.

Sources: Jack Shulimson, *U.S. Marines in Vietnam: An Expanding War, 1966* (Washington, DC: US Marine Corps Headquarters History and Museums Division, 1982), 1982), chapter 8, quote on page 127, https://archive.org/details/usmarinesinvietn00jack_0; Operation Texas, 20 March 1966, Folder 063, US Marine Corps History Division Vietnam War Documents Collection, The Vietnam Center and Archive, Texas Tech University, www.vietnam.ttu.edu/virtualarchive/items.php?item=1201063064.

TWELVE

Homeward Bound

My orders arrived out of the blue. I packed up my belongings and was taken to a large staging building in preparation for the flight home. Good-byes were brief, and I wasted no time getting to where I was supposed to be. There was no way that I was going to miss my ride. I almost got myself court-martialed some weeks earlier when a fellow corpsman whom I had visited Saigon with received his orders to go home. We were still at the Chu Lai location at that time, and he was on a tight schedule to catch a ride up north to Da Nang. The individual who processed my friend's paperwork for his transfer orders was in no hurry to get him on his way; after all, the paper pusher wasn't going anywhere, so why should he hurry? The way things were progressing, my friend was going to miss the transportation out of Chu Lai that day.

Not only did this corpsman report to me, but in some ways I was like an older brother to him. I approached the corpsman who was processing the orders and who happened to be senior to me in rank. I asked him about getting my buddy out that morning. He gave me some flippant reply that he had other stuff to do, too. My mind ventured into the danger zone, and I informed him that if my buddy missed his ride out of here, that he personally would get his ass kicked—or words to that effect. I knew full well that this is not a wise thing to do in the military, so I sat down on my cot waiting for our chief petty officer to call me over to his tent. Sure enough, the person who was working on the orders did report me, and over I went to see the chief. I was one of the more experienced field medical corpsman and had more field experience than most any other corpsman in the battalion. Maybe that would count for something. The chief asked a few questions, and I told him the circumstances surrounding my out-of-character behavior. He chewed me out for what I had said, after which he called over the petty officer who was processing the orders and told him to get them done now or else.

My friend made it to his ride to Da Nang that day. The person typing up the orders had nothing to say to me afterward, and I gave him every chance to speak up, believe me. I should not have been so cocky, but I offer no apology for my actions. I was thankful that the chief petty officer used his discretion not to throw the book at me. I think he was a good enough manager to know that I intended to see that my buddy was going home that day no matter what I had to do to get it done. He was right.

The time in Da Nang was largely a negative experience and generally a downer. I have no idea what I expected, but I was not nearly as happy to be leaving as I should have been. Possibly it had something to do with leaving behind my corpsmen buddies and the marines with whom I spent all of my time, including some guys who had been in country as long as I had. Maybe I wanted to be the last one out, which stirred pangs of guilt. We came here en masse, but we left as individuals, either walking out or being carried. All of the experiences in Vietnam that appear in this book were shared with others.

I did eventually catch my plane after maybe a month at Da Nang. It was surreal to be leaving South Vietnam. I don't think that I believed it was happening until we were airborne.

We stopped over in Okinawa for a few days, getting processed for our eventual return to the States. I took this time to spend some of the money I had saved. For a year I basically spent nothing, except for my trip to Saigon. I had it all planned out as I shopped my way through the huge military store. A large reel-to-reel Akai tape recorder and some high-quality tailored suits for me, a good set of Noritake china for my mother, a 35mm camera for my dad, and some smaller gifts for my siblings were all shipped home directly from the store.

I took some liberty time to return up to the little bar that I had frequented before we departed for Vietnam. The same woman was in charge of the bar, and she said that the young lady I was looking for had left for nursing school. I think we would have had a good time, but I was glad she was doing something positive with herself. I had a good time anyway, and I basically chilled out, listening to some music on the jukebox, and drinking a few *cold* beers. Beer was served warm, even hot, in Vietnam since ice and refrigerators were not available. I was just glad to be sitting here.

The military guys on the base largely left the returning vets alone about the war. I could tell they wanted to know what they could expect when they got over there, but they didn't ask. Some of those coming back told a few stories, but most did not, leaving well enough alone. The guys going to Vietnam understood. I felt their anxiety, especially since they would be there in short order. No ships or delays, but a quick plane ride into a whole new world. By now, everybody knew what might be in store, and they didn't need to hear the kind of details we didn't want to talk about anyway.

No one spoke to us about anything resembling posttraumatic stress disorder (PTSD). That diagnostic term was not recognized by mental health professionals until 1980. Except for visiting with a chaplain or possibly a medical doctor, no counseling took place. It was expected that we would just slip right back into the routine way of life as if nothing had happened the past twelve months to change our outlook. The closest thing discussed in those days came was when someone thought a returning person was possibly exhibiting symptoms of "combat fatigue," and even that was perceived as an oddity. That was something that happened in World War II, like "shell shock" during World War I. Maybe the experts figured that Vietnam wasn't as extreme a situation as a world war. Perhaps medical treatment was available for mental and emotional issues that surfaced later on, but I didn't know about it. There were no preventive counseling efforts that I saw to help us readjust. "Time cures all" was the prevailing attitude. The world sure as hell wasn't going to wait for us to catch up to where we had left off.

Looking back on these circumstances, I can understand them to some degree, because I personally was not looking to open up about anything that was bothering me. I just wanted to go home for a while. I didn't care to talk to anyone about the war or dwell on what happened in Vietnam—or did I really want to scream out at the top of my lungs about all of it? The military culture didn't foster an attitude of talking over problems, but solving them yourself. I am sure that if they were offered an adequate, private, and confidential opportunity, plenty of jarheads would have opened up about their personal issues. I personally had no expectation of privacy in the service, whether it was with a chaplain or a doctor. Remember the posting of the names in the mess hall of those having venereal disease?

In my case, it wasn't that I wanted to forget the experience or pretend it didn't happen. I put it in its place and was ready to move on. I believe my psychologist daughter would say that I exhibited compartmentalized behavior. It would have been good to have a formal program for helping the personnel going home to at least talk with them about what they might expect. Present-day attitudes are much improved concerning exposure to traumatic stress than in the sixties and seventies. At least I sure as hell hope so. I don't believe there is a stigma of shame surrounding such issues in today's world. I'm not nearly as sure about the causes of this stress being addressed, however.

At least returning troops today don't have to be ashamed of their wartime experiences, such as we were supposed to be, according to some of the hate-filled demonstrators who spent their time getting in front of any television camera that would film them. We didn't know exactly what to expect when we got home. Personally I was not worried about what anyone else thought, and I would deal with it accordingly.

After a few days in Okinawa, off to California we flew, ready or not, while some of our troops headed toward battle. I found myself wondering whether someone or something was going to come along and screw this up, but after a lengthy trip, the plane landed and we quietly walked back into civilization. Being tossed into the hustle of California in the mid-1960s as if nothing had changed at all from when I had been stationed there some years earlier was a peculiar homecoming. I had changed, but the changes in California were much too subtle for me to recognize. I had considerable leave time coming to me, so I headed home to Nebraska with an inner groundswell of anticipation along with just a hint of anxiety. I knew that my family would be extremely glad to see me, but I had not come close to leaving Vietnam behind. My mind needed to catch up with my body. I surprised myself in that I was able to recognize this issue and deal with it in a reasonable manner that worked for me.

I had a great homecoming with my family. Not all of us could be together at that time, though. One of my younger brothers was also in the navy, but thankfully not in Vietnam, nor anywhere near it. My youngest brother would be going on active duty in the navy later that year, and my now not so little sister was busy with her high school activities. Both my parents had aged, and it hit home that the past year was hard on everyone. They had their own share of problems to reckon with besides worrying about me while I was gone.

I experienced no monumental problems readjusting to a normal routine. We were always a tight-knit and loving family, even if we didn't wear it on our sleeves. When six people live in small houses for most of their lives, there is a lot of interaction, and we still nearly always had our evening meal together. That was our social hour, and still no one was allowed to ignore the rest of us. I had a couple of weeks to recoup what sanity I had left, and it was very good to be back not only in my own country and in Nebraska, but most of all, in my own home. How fortunate I was to have a family and a hometown like mine. I wondered if my marines and fellow corpsmen had similar reunions. I hoped that they had the very best. The midwestern friendliness and the good-natured ways of its people made it easy for me to almost believe that I hadn't been gone at all. One thing that stood out was that I was a very dirty brown from the days of heat and filth baked into my pores, but nothing that time and a little scrubbing wouldn't handle. I definitely had my summer tan on early that year.

Everyone welcomed me back home in a positive way. Even though our family had only moved to this little farming community at the beginning of my senior year in high school, I knew just about everybody in town. That was the way it was. Sort of like our own family, everybody knew a little about each other's business. This was especially good if you were on the positive side of the gossip mill, but maybe not so great if you slipped out of line or were in trouble. My dad would kid around about the occasional lack of privacy, but it was the same way in my birthplace in Kansas where most of my relatives lived. Small-town life doesn't have a monopoly on generosity, but if someone was in need, there was no hesitation from the townspeople to lend a helping hand any way they could. I did visit my relatives in Kansas, but I spent the majority of my time soaking in my immediate family, whom I had missed dearly the past eighteen months.

During my leave home I had a hard time buying my own beer at the local tavern, because no one would let me pay. I was one of the first, but by no means the last, from the local area to serve in South Vietnam. No matter what their personal beliefs were, no one I knew then or know now would have ever looked down upon the troops like they apparently did in some other parts of the country, especially later in the war. Some of the younger guys wanted to know all the details of what went on, and the older guys who bought me beer wanted to tell me what it was all about. Sometimes just walking down the main street sidewalk was a humbling experience, because then some of the townspeople would offer more of an emotional welcome back and comment about how my family worried about my safety when I was gone. It was very difficult emotionally for me to hear firsthand about how hard it was on my family. They were the last people on earth I would have wanted to hurt, and they didn't burden me by constantly reminding me of their concerns.

I made it a point not to consume so many beers that I was tempted to start telling war stories. Possibly that is exactly what I was wanting to do, but I didn't know how to go about it honorably. A part of me wanted to talk and get things off my chest, but I didn't do it. I don't think that I really knew where to begin. I didn't strut around town in my uniform, and I didn't want to shame any part of being in the military by acting like a fool in public. The Vietnam conflict was still a relatively novel but dominating event, and no one had any idea that it would go on for nine more years.

There were antiwar protests, but in the Midwest I think the prevailing attitude was that there was a job to do, let's do it right. No one had to be there to have an opinion. Even some draft-dodging college kid protesting what we were doing over there had a right to express his opinion, and it took all the understanding I could marshal to listen to it and read about it. There were more misconceptions about what was happening in Vietnam than any well-grounded understanding. I couldn't do much about this, and I don't think that I knew how to put it right in any case. Instead, I decided at the time to not get all twisted around within the debate, but to focus on putting my future back on the right track after I was released from active duty in August.

I never forgot about the guys who were still over there, and I was reminded every night on TV that "out of sight, out of mind" was not going to happen. I made it a goal not to overindulge on the television news, but I kept current. For a while, I entertained thoughts of returning to Vietnam for another tour. Part of this was guilt for leaving the others there, and part of it was guilt for not getting the job finished. My hitch was coming to a close, and I would have had to reenlist to do this, which was not a price I was willing to pay. I didn't really have the guts to go back anyway, and I genuinely wanted to stay right here in my own country. In some cases, guys did go back for another tour of duty. I heard that some did it for the money, and in rare cases people actually wanted to participate in the action. I imagine that for an even rarer few it was a rush for them. The sad thing for me is that I understand where those guys were coming from, too.

While on leave, I took time to register for college classes, which began in a few months. I found a small room to rent off campus with one of the nicest elderly landladies a person could find. Being a veteran, I could live off campus as a freshman, and I didn't have to take physical education. I was eligible for the educational benefits from the GI Bill of Rights, which actually made it financially possible for me to attend college without having a job during the school year. I had taken a few classes at the University of Hawaii while I was stationed there, so I had an inkling of what college coursework was like, which made me even more anxious to get started. With help from my dad, I purchased a car with my savings. It was a beautiful car, in my humble opinion, and only four years old. It had a 327-cubic-inch engine with dual carbs and plenty of horsepower, which made it a respectably fast Chevy even for those days. By the grace of God, I had arrived. I had waited a long time to get my hands on a car like this one. The days on leave passed by quickly, and soon it was time to travel to my next and my last active-duty military assignment, which was about five hundred miles due east.

THIRTEEN

Becoming a Sailor Once Again?

I was going to be stationed at the Great Lakes Naval Hospital, which was part of the large US naval base near Waukegan, Illinois. While I was still in Vietnam, President Johnson extended everyone's active-duty portion of their military commitment by four more months. This was necessary for meeting the manpower requirements of the military, as it was explained to us at the time. For four years I practically counted down the days until July 30, 1966, when I would get out, but now it was officially four more months. At first I was infuriated that this was about to happen, then I was relieved to know that the four months would not be added on to my tour in Vietnam. That helped, and I was going to apply for an early release from active duty anyway because of attending college. I hoped that it would get approved so that I could attend classes in the fall.

I remember thinking as I was driving my new car from Nebraska to Illinois that I had a lot to look forward to and be thankful for. With the radio blaring out the hits from the sixties it was almost as if I was back in the good ol' high school days, but missing of course was the innocence of a time impossible to recapture. I'd been through a lot for a twenty-one-year-old, but I was still a young man and had a lot to learn about making my own way. The military had always made sure I was fed and had a place to sleep, and medical treatment was always available. They took care of my physical needs, and not too long from now, these responsibilities would fall on my own shoulders in a real sense. I couldn't wait to begin this part of my life.

The first thing I did when I arrived at Great Lakes was to apply for an early out, which was a program designed for veterans who had a legitimate reason for early release from active duty. If I could prove that I was going to attend classes full time, being granted an early out was almost a sure thing. The end result was that I had my request approved, and the four months were adjusted back so that I would be released from active-duty status in late August, three days before classes began. I guess if guys could get a college deferment to avoid being drafted, then I could get out early to begin college classes.

The second thing I did at Great Lakes was to buy some new uniforms. I was back in the navy now, and my original naval uniforms were too small and had the wrong rank insignia from three years earlier. I had the option of wearing either uniform, depending on the circumstances or event, so I wore my marine uniform some of the time and navy whites other times. Sometimes it just depended on my mood. Did I feel like a marine or like a sailor that day? No one cared either way.

The Great Lakes Naval Hospital was a very impressive facility. Some fifteen stories tall, it dominated the area as the centerpiece of this portion of the base complex. It was a beehive of activity and an integral part of a congested area comprising civilians and sailors carrying out their daily work duties. Close by was the Great Lakes Naval Recruitment Training Center, where my youngest brother would be stationed for boot camp. Waukegan and the surrounding area offered an interesting mix of military and civilian influences. This was as close to a civilian job as I was going to get and still be in the military, even more so than when I was in California attending hospital corps school. On some level I understood why some people reenlisted, especially if they could secure duty like this on a regular basis. Even the food was outstanding, but my focus never wavered and steadfastly remained on returning to civilian life and starting college in the fall.

Out of all the places in the hospital I could have pulled duty, they assigned me to work in the emergency room. It worked out all right in the end, and I learned a great deal in assisting with unusual and serious medical cases. One thing I hadn't counted on was that every couple of weeks a bus or two loaded with US Marine Corps casualties from Vietnam arrived for longer-term medical treatment or further transfer. They were checked in and admitted through the emergency room facilities. I was just barely back from Vietnam myself, and I was seeing guys who made it back but who were not in good shape—at least not yet. This situation didn't help much with trying to get Vietnam off my mind, but I think it may have been helpful in subtler ways. I now didn't feel quite as much as if I had abandoned those still over there. The cord to those still in Vietnam was not cut completely, and that was probably a good thing for my own mental well-being. Maybe I was getting nearer to where I had begun my journey four years ago. Many years later I realize that the cord will never be completely severed.

A few of these guys on occasion had a negative attitude toward some of the hospital personnel who were helping them. Some of this was that old navy-versus-marine animosity rearing its ugly head again. Part of it stemmed from the fact that they were desperately searching for someone to understand their situation. They were hurting, and the last thing they needed was sympathy, but they didn't necessarily understand that. It was good to see these guys, and on occasion I wore my marine uniform with my ribbons indicating my Vietnam experiences. That immediately broke down any communication barrier or any feelings of their being all alone, and I think it may have temporarily helped with the attitudes. It definitely did not hurt for them to be able to identify with someone who had been in combat, and I hoped and prayed that it somehow helped them to a faster recovery. In fairness to all of the navy corpsmen who worked with these patients, I never once heard a negative comment or complaint about the marines, only a very caring approach. I wasn't the least bit surprised that all of the corpsmen were a class act all their own, in addition to being very understanding.

I have good memories from Great Lakes for a variety of reasons, but I was on cruise control militarily, and I spent my free time thinking about the end of August. I went up to Milwaukee and down to Chicago sightseeing and getting acclimated to normal life. I enjoyed working in such a large and beautiful hospital. Everyone treated me well, but I never felt completely at ease. Maybe it was too quiet, but it seemed that I was looking for something that I hadn't yet found or was waiting for something to happen that wasn't going to happen. My parents even drove out to visit me for a weekend. I'm not sure my dad or mom had ever been on a military base, but they were on a nice one now. It was a neat thing for my parents to do, and we had a good time just seeing the area like tourists. We were all trying to make up for lost time by being together.

One morning my chief corpsman told me to get in my dress uniform along with ribbons, and report over to the large assembly hall on base. Once over there I learned that there were going to be award presentations by the captain, who was in command of all medical personnel. There I sat on this large stage along with some other sailors in front of what looked like the whole base. After everyone quieted down, the captain made a few announcements and remarks, then read a citation relating to my actions during the last major operation in which my company and I participated (see Figure 13.1).

He then presented me with a Gold Star in lieu of a second Bronze Star Medal with Combat V for valor. The crowd roared its approval and gave me a standing ovation, the likes of which I will never again experience. I was appreciative and caught totally off guard by this event. I didn't know it was coming, nor did I know that I was recommended for the award. I don't know who would have written this documentation, since my original first sergeant had been transferred out of our unit prior to this particular mission. It was likely the first lieutenant in charge who made the recommendation. It didn't really matter, for here I was. As I stood on the stage looking out at their faces, I was thinking it might inspire or at least give some insight to my fellow corpsmen and hospital corps school students, who had not been to Vietnam. Mostly, I wanted them to think, *If this guy can do it, so can I.* To say I wasn't proud to be standing up there in front of my peers would be a lie.

Part of the routine procedure for the navy, as it likely is for all branches of the military, is to have an exit interview with a senior non-commissioned officer, to receive all one's discharge information and paperwork, and to get the reenlistment talk. In my case the navy representative gave me all of my information and told me that I would still be in the inactive reserves for a couple of more years. He got to the part about reenlistment, talked about a promotion if I were to reenlist, and

UNITED STATES MARINE CORPS
HEADQUARTERS, FLEET MARINE FORCE, PACIFIC
FPO, SAN FRANCISCO. 96602

In the name of the President of the United States, the Commanding General, Fleet Marine Force, Pacific takes pleasure in presenting a gold star in lieu of the second BRONZE STAR MEDAL to

HOSPITAL CORPSMAN THIRD CLASS RICHARD WARREN SCHAEFER

UNITED STATES NAVY

for service as set forth in the following

CITATION:

"For heroic achievement in connection with operations against insurgent communist (Viet Cong) forces in the Republic of Vietnam while serving with Company E, Second Battalion, Fourth Marines. On 21 March 1966, Hospital Corpsman SCHAEFER was attached to a platoon participating in a search and destroy operation near Quang Ngai. As the platoon approached to within thirty-five meters of a village they were taken under fire by a large Viet Cong force located in heavily fortified positions and trench lines which encircled the entire village. Within a short period of time, the intense enemy fire had inflicted heavy casualties on the platoon, the majority of which were located in an exposed rice paddy directly in front of the enemy positions. Without hesitation and with complete disregard for his own safety, Hospital Corpsman SCHAEFER proceeded to administer aid to the fallen Marines. Seemingly oblivious to the volume of fire around him, Hospital Corpsman SCHAEFER calmly and quickly performed his duties until each and every wounded man had been evacuated, carrying out several himself. His exceptional courage and tireless devotion to duty throughout the engagement were in keeping with the highest traditions of the United States Naval Service."

Hospital Corpsman SCHAEFER is authorized to wear the Combat "V".

FOR THE PRESIDENT,

V. H. KRULAK
LIEUTENANT GENERAL, U. S. MARINE CORPS
COMMANDING

TEMPORARY CITATION

13.1 Citation for a Gold Star in lieu of the second Bronze Star Medal relating to combat operations on March 21, 1966. Courtesy of United States Marine Corps

Grandson Of Localites Is Awarded Gold Star For Service In Vietnam

1966

Hospital Corpsman Richard W. Schaefer, formerly of Marysville was presented a gold star in lieu of the second Bronze Star medal and a citation for heroic action in Vietnam.

The citation in part: "For heroic achievement in the Republic of Vietnam while serving with Company E, Second Battalion, Fourth Marines. On March 21, 1966, Hospital Corpsman Schaefer was attached to a platoon participating near Quang Nagai. As the platoon approached a village they were taken under fire by a large Viet Cong force which encircled the entire village. Within a short period of time, the intense enemy fire had inflicted heavy casualties on the platoon, the majority of which were located directly in front of the enemy positions. Without hesitation and with complete disregard for his own safety, Hospital Corpsman Schaefer preceded to administer aid to the fallen Marines. Seemingly oblivious of the volume of fire around him, Hospital Corpsman Schaefer performed his duties until each and every wounded man had been evacuated, carrying out several himself. His exceptional courage and tireless devotion to duty throughout the engagement were in the keeping with the highest traditions of the United States Naval Service."

RICHARD SCHAEFER

Hospital Corpsman Schaefer is authorized to wear the Combat "V."

During his four years in the U.S. Navy, he served three years as a field hospital corpsman with the Marine Corps.

In addition to the bronze stars, he received the Purple Heart, Good Conduct medal, Navy Unit citation. Vietnamese Expeditionary, and National Defense awards.

He is now enrolled at Wayne State college, Wayne, Neb., and is the son of Mr. and Mrs. Irvin Schaefer, Hooper, Neb., formerly of Marysville. He is also the grandson of Mr. and Mrs. Geo. Schaefer, Herkimer, and Mr. and Mrs. Ben Hildebrandt, Marysville.

13.2 The newspapers in both of my hometowns kept track of us in the military, sometimes with a little help from Mom and Dad. Courtesy of *Marysville* (KS) *Advocate*. Photo from author's collection.

then he noticed that I was getting an early out for school, even though it was one month past my original July release date. He remarked, "I guess you won't be reenlisting." I confirmed that, thanked him, and made for the door. My seabags were already packed, one with my navy uniforms and one with my marine uniforms. *Where's the band? Where is the grand exit party?* I thought to myself as I left his office. It felt anticlimactic.

My youngest brother took his first plane ride out to ride back home with me. I don't believe he knew at the time that he would be back at Great Lakes in a few months. He had already signed up with the navy, and he would be leaving home as he neared his eighteenth birthday. We didn't spend much time around the base, particularly since I began school in a few days, but we enjoyed the ride back together and I definitely appreciated his company. The way it worked out is that I was leaving active duty, and he was about to begin. All three of us brothers were in at the same time, and the colleges were jammed with young men sweating it out with their deferments. Once, as I recall, I met up with my older younger brother in San Diego. We had a nice visit, and I remember him being proud of the ship that he was stationed on, which was docked there. Down deep I hated it that my brothers had to enlist, but I was proud of them. No one was complaining out loud. It was an odd time for our country. Nothing made a lot of logical sense. With my civilian clothes hanging from a clothes bar over the backseat of the car, we pointed the hood of the Chevy into the afternoon sun and headed due west, straight for Nebraska.

For the first time in over four years I felt free—free to go where I wished and free to live and work anywhere I pleased. No more liberty requests. No more going to jail for telling the boss off, not that I would ever do that. I still had two years of inactive reserve status to complete before I would receive my final discharge from the navy, but the chance of being called up for active duty was slim. I arrived back home and started my college classes four years later than I had originally wanted.

College was almost everything I had imagined it would be. I found my coursework interesting and challenging, and I kept busy with all things college. I was older by a few years than most of my classmates, but it was never a problem. Since I hadn't ever developed good study habits,

I had to address that right from the start. Some of the college kids were so into themselves that they came off as boorish. I have to admit that I had to learn to relax and take things in stride, and maybe they were just serious students. I didn't have a lot of heavy responsibilities other than to myself. Even though I was happy and grateful to be in my present position, I was still wrapped a little tight. Over time, I began to unwind a bit and focus on the things at hand. I realized I had to change; it wasn't the college atmosphere's responsibility to change for me. I was determined that what happened in Vietnam was not going to control my behavior or my outlook. I was in control, or so I thought.

A fellow student who also rented a room in the house I lived in became a good friend. He was an upperclassman, so our maturity levels along with some common interests made it easy to get along well. I would say that he was my first civilian friend since leaving the service. He was someone to talk to, which was important to me. I had been around a lot of people day and night for four years, and now it was not difficult to feel lonely.

Never on campus, or anywhere else for that matter, did I witness any antiwar rhetoric or demonstrations. I was not the only veteran on the beautiful Wayne State College campus of three thousand students in Wayne, Nebraska, and I don't remember any issues concerning my military service.

Many of the professors were liberal in their views, but that was fine with me, since I was reared a free spirit and was hungry to hear other points of view. One of my most interesting professors was in the sociology department, and more than any of my other professors he promoted thought and empathy concerning the good of our fellow man. My history professor attempted to provoke thought, too, but unfortunately his ego was so lost in his own interpretation of history that he lost my interest halfway through the semester. I'm not sure whether he even knew the time period in which he was living.

Wayne a small county-seat community about the same size as where I was brought up in Kansas. Since I wasn't looking for a high-energy setting, the peace, calm, and beauty of our little campus were fine with me for the time being. It was probably a very good place for me personally in

OCTOBER 27. 1966

WAR HERO RICHARD SCHAEFER BUYS STAMP

First sale of the new 5-cent stamps honoring American servicemen was made by Postal Clerk Leo Corbin to Richard Schaefer, Viet Nam war hero, who is now attending Wayne State College.

Hospital Corpsman Schaefer was presented a Gold Star in lieu of a second Bronze Star and a citation for heroic action in Viet Nam. In addition to the Bronze Stars, he has the Purple Heart, Good Conduct Medal, Navy Unit Citation, Vietnamese Expeditionary, and National Defense Awards.

Richard, son of Mr. and Mrs. Irvin Schaefer, served four years in the Navy, three years as a field Hospital Corpsman with the Marine Corps.

New 5¢ Postage Stamps Go On Sale Today

A 5-Cent stamp honoring American servicemen and marking the 25th anniversary of the Savings Bond program was first placed on sale on Oct. 26 at Sioux City, Iowa, where students of the North Junior High School conceived the idea for a patriotic stamp in tribue to our servicemen.

Postmaster Clarence Heywood states that the stamp was designed by Steven Dohonos, a member of the Citizens' Stamp Advisory Committee. Mr. Dohanos based his design on a photograph of the Flag and Statute of Liberty by Bob Noble, which appeared in the New York Herald-Tribune on Oct. 29, 1961.

The blue lettering "United States Savings Bonds" and the sky were printed by lithography. The Giori presses printed the dark blue field of the Flag, red for stripes, denomination and lettering "We appreciate our Servicemen" and black for the Statue of Liberty and wording "25th Anniversary".

13.3 I was asked to help promote a new five-cent postage stamp honoring military personnel. I would have preferred not to say "war hero" in the article, but the newspaper strongly supported our military over the years. I would never take that for granted. Courtesy of *Hooper* (NE) *Sentinel*, presently the *Rustler Sentinel* (Hooper, Nebraska).

more ways that I could have appreciated at the time. I was grateful to be attending college—a dream of mine for a long time.

I was transitioning back to civilian life, even though I occasionally fought an internal, emotional tug of war. Part of me wanted to put the military out of my mind, yet part of me wanted to retain the desirable traits that I believe the military added to my personality. It was a work in progress.

FOURTEEN

Thoughts on the Past, Hopes for the Future

I thought long and hard about my rationale for writing this last chapter. Does anyone still think about the Vietnam War that dominated our attention so long ago? Does anyone actually care about our treatment of the returning troops or the perception of the military way back then? After all, we appear to be treating the military in a respectful manner today. I came to the conclusion that I still cared enough to offer my point of view, and I believe that others care as well. The comments that I make in this chapter are mine alone. I am not a politician, a military authority, or a historian with expertise relative to Vietnam. My role was that of a participant in a conflict larger than the war itself.

One comment in particular that irritates me and undoubtedly many other Vietnam veterans is when someone all knowingly proclaims, "Yeah, that was the only war the US has ever lost." In my estimation this assertion is grossly oversimplified and based upon embryonic reasoning. Any failures associated with Vietnam fall largely on the shoulders of the politicians, both ours and South Vietnam's, including the senior military leadership who together formulated our foreign policy and provided direction at that particular time in history. Our military didn't directly lose anything to the Viet Cong or North Vietnamese military forces. We weren't allowed to pursue the enemy to all of their known locations, and we carried out orders just like in any other war in which our country was ever involved, albeit with more restrictions placed upon us. We in the peon ranks weren't necessarily aware of what the limitations entailed and the reasons for them, but we wondered about the politics of the war just the same. We didn't have the luxury of protesting such policies, but instead we carried them out on our backs—not blindly, but dutifully.

The Vietnam War was complex, and no one had or has all the answers. There was no war lost and no war won, but only a shell of a country that became so infected with ideological strife that its people could no longer overcome it, once their protection—their only allies—had left. We, along with a handful of other countries, were their protection. No one was there when their villages were under siege by the insurgents during the night. Try as they might, the South Vietnamese military forces weren't enough to stave off their enemies. To those who insist that we lost the war, I only request that they may reconsider their viewpoints someday. I also hope that they don't feel the same way about our efforts in Iraq and Afghanistan because things do not go perfectly smoothly as countries struggle to survive on their own under their respective forms of government. Our military mission was accomplished every day as we put forth the effort to help and protect those we came to Vietnam to assist.

Many of the veterans who were featured in the local newspaper series I described earlier in this book expressed the opinion that we could have had a more successful conclusion to our efforts if we had given it more time, had fewer restrictions on engagements, and retained better support back home. I am not sure that I agree with extending the war. I believed that we were doing the right thing by being there, just as most of them did. I do not know if those in charge understood that the South Vietnamese could not win the fight for their country, but it appears that they did not judge the strengths of either side correctly.

There were no clear-cut battle lines drawn, with enemy forces on one side and us on the other. There was no country to capture. The enemy may be the farmer who smiled at us during the day and then would slit our throats during the night if he had the means to do it. He may have been the farmer who along with his friends from some of the other villages banded together and threatened their own neighbors, including women and children, with death if they didn't follow along. He probably believed deeply in what the insurgency and the North Vietnamese leader, Ho Chi Minh, were promoting. Or the enemy may have been the woman who lost many of her relatives to all the years of discord and war that she had seen nearly all of her life. Perhaps she and her family were threatened with bodily harm after we left her unprotected and therefore she had no choice but to support our opponents. This would be her payment for protection, similar to the protection the mob offered shopkeepers in Chicago during the 1920s, at least in my estimation. The dynamics were complex and difficult for anyone to comprehend. I came to the belief that some of these people no doubt became lost in the longer-term despair of it all. Who in the hell wouldn't have?

At that time in history, our country had been in extensive military actions in almost every decade of the twentieth century, stopping only during the 1920s and 1930s: the Philippine War in the '00s, World War I in the '10s, World War II in the '40s, and Korea in the '50s. Throw in the Bay of Pigs, the Soviet nuclear war threat, and a few other worldly problems, and we have a country that did not want to hear about another war on the horizon. When the citizenry discovered that we were going to engage in a regionalized conflict in South Vietnam, for an unspecified amount of time and with an undetermined cost of American lives, they understandably pushed back. Add in the anxiety effect of the draft on college-age males, and it was no surprise that there were protests against the war in Vietnam. Not only did those protesting the war have the constitutional right to protest, but they had a legitimate right to voice their concerns.

My own father didn't believe that we should be in Vietnam. The main difference between him and my mother was that Dad didn't want *any* of us over there, while Mom didn't want *me and my brothers* over there. On a larger scale, it seemed as if there were two sets of protestors at the same time. One group protested the involvement in Vietnam but supported our military, while the other group protested and demonstrated against not only the war but the military and any authority figure. These two groups were not ideologically united. In fact I doubt many of them would care to be around each other in private settings. As the war dragged on, the costs were becoming too high, and there was no clear end in sight. Most people began to come to this conclusion.

What the protestors and demonstrators did not have a right to do, in my opinion, was to sit on antiaircraft weapons in North Vietnam belittling our country, like one or two of our more beloved movie starlets did. While they obviously have the right of freedom of expression, I don't believe this right includes providing aid and comfort to an enemy of the United States. The North Vietnamese used these visiting protestors like pawns for their political and possibly military gain. I forgave Jane Fonda years ago for her error in judgment, but it cannot be forgotten. I do not believe that the protestors had the right to spit on returning veterans or refer to them as baby killers and murderers. Furthermore, the protestors did not have the right to turn their backs on or blame our troops for our involvement in South Vietnam. My view is that people had a responsibility, at the very least, to leave the military personnel returning home alone and not harass them without at least trying to comprehend what they might be experiencing.

Somehow the protests against the policies of our civilian leadership were transferred, at least in part—intentionally or not—to the military personnel. Those of us in Vietnam could understand the difference between protesting political decisions and protesting against us. This is why some began feeling betrayed by those who should have been supporting us. It was challenging enough to maintain a positive attitude about our mission, let alone hear from back home that many people didn't support the war, or us for that matter. It was the perfect stage for making us feel like it was indeed a "lonely war." I think many Vietnam veterans carry this perception with them even to this day.

Vocal public opinion and the press together enabled this transformation to gain momentum and create the perception that made it a shameful thing to wear a military uniform in public. I think that we would want our military to have a little swagger and be proud to display our country's uniform. My youngest brother told me that officials warned his unit not to wear their uniforms out in public, but to wear civilian attire while off the base or traveling. That should never have happened. This did not deter my brothers and me from wearing our uniforms anywhere and anytime we wanted to. I think this was especially true in the case of the brother closer in age to me, who didn't care a whole lot about other people's opinions on such matters. He was proud of the fact that he could wear the uniform. The confidence and support our military had always enjoyed had eroded, and in my opinion, it would take until President Reagan took office to regain what should never have been such a lost pride. The rest of the world probably saw us as confused and stumbling. I believe to this day that this was a dangerous image for us to portray as a country over such a long period of time and that it weakened our national resolve.

Since Vietnam, there were nearly two relatively quiet decades—that is, until Iraq, Bosnia, and then Iraq once again and Afghanistan came into view. The reasons for our presence in these countries may be vastly different than for Vietnam, but there are noticeable parallels nevertheless. Going from village to village and back again attempting to convince a population that we are there to help them—and that other forces attempting to influence them are wrong—has a familiar ring to it. So do: "We are in it for the long haul." "We won't desert them if they stand up for their rights; in fact, we will help train them to do that." "We're not in the business of nation-building." Have we not heard this all before? We need to stay the course, but we also need to learn from history and think carefully about our goals. Strategic end objectives must be clearly stated, and I am sure this is not always the case today.

Looking ahead, my opinion is that we need to be very resourceful about how we utilize our military personnel and not treat them as some sort of renewable resource. Our country has to find a way that the local pizza parlor manager who serves in the National Guard does not have to serve multiple tours of duty in combat areas. I will not let my intelligence be insulted by believing that a surge of thirty thousand troops saved the day in Iraq, as some of our politicians asserted. National Guard troops served in the Vietnam period, but I don't think they were abused to the point they are today. This puts more pressure on them and the active-duty forces as well. If we keep this up we should not be surprised at the number of posttraumatic stress disorder cases or suicides of returning veterans. Multiple tours of duty in combat areas may contribute directly to increases in PTSD cases. The troops are being worn down mentally, not physically. They undergo routine physical fitness tests, but

I doubt that psychological reviews take place for everyone returning to combat duty. One part of the emotional response after leaving a combat zone is feeling grateful that you have escaped an environment where someone was trying to kill you. I base this comment on my own experience. The last thing I would have wanted to hear six months after leaving Vietnam is that I would be ordered to go back for another tour of duty.

Perhaps we are not as strong as we should be from a troop-level standpoint. If so, we cannot bluff about this position and win, especially if other countries sense our situation. We can ill afford to rely only on our technology. We have an endpoint in this area, because we will not use our most devastating technological deterrents—nuclear weapons—and every sane person knows it. Therefore, we need to ensure that we have superior conventional warfare personnel and equipment to deter others and to defend ourselves in any event. We must be unequivocally prepared for any contingency.

I would be against a return to drafting our military personnel, but we do need to assess where we are and make some improvements in troop allotments. As a country we appear to be very supportive of our troops, but I maintain a skeptical eye regarding what would happen if the draft was reinstated. At the present time it is convenient to have an all-volunteer military, which means that the average citizen does not have to get directly involved if they wish not to. Cheering on our troops from a distance is not difficult. What will be our attitude when a real time commitment has to be made? What if conditions result in things hitting close to home? As in my personal case and as many of the veterans stated in the newspaper series, we volunteered to enlist to get it over with.

As it stands now, all men between the ages of eighteen and twenty-five are required to register with the Selective Service System. Women are not yet required to register. I understand that this system was left in place in the event we ever choose to implement a military draft again to fulfill national manpower needs. If we cannot arrive at the numbers deemed adequate by recruiting volunteers, then our choice may very well be a reinstatement of the draft. One thing that I am not concerned about regarding future military needs is the ability of the young people who will have to carry the load. Future generations will do a fine job relative to whatever they are called upon to do. We can see this every day if we just look around. The young people of today are stronger, smarter, and in my opinion, more worldly than those of us who preceded them.

Having a superior military force is a fundamental element in dealing with our international woes, but it isn't intended to be a cure-all for solving our problems. How many times since the terrible events of September 11, 2001, have we been advised that we must be vigilant, remain alert, report unusual behavior, and always stay aware of our surroundings? A steady diet of these comments has been fed to us, including our young people, for years now. This advice is well intended and probably good for all of us to remember, as long as we also remember to keep things in context. I grew up fearing and hating all things Russia. I do not want my grandsons growing up fearing or hating all Middle Eastern countries and their people.

This is not to imply that we can ignore threats from such entities as the Islamic State caliphate (ISIL or ISIS). They are making life miserable for a number of countries in the Middle East and elsewhere by their extreme cruelty and ruthless tactics. These people have an explicit wish and a capability to do us harm, even within our own borders. It is well beyond the scope of this book and my expertise to delve into discussions pertaining to terrorism and the host of foreign affairs issues we face. Our way of life has been altered since 9/11, but we need not live in fear waiting for the other shoe to drop. If something bad happens to us, we will deal with it and move on. This concept is not new for us. It will take time, but we will succeed and get better at subjugating these threats along with those attempting to make good on them.

For all who may have bumper stickers showing ribbons and flags supporting our troops, and for those who wear flag pins on their clothing or have flags proudly displayed at their homes, I request only that we stay committed. Those in the military service are obviously going to need us behind them for the long haul we have ahead. One person whom I would wager has bumper stickers indicating support of our troops is one of my military buddies from Louisiana. I knew him and his wife from our days in Hawaii, and we were stationed together through our time in Vietnam. He was working primarily in the battalion aid station while I was attached to an infantry company, but we never lost touch. We had the type of relationship where the second we would see each other again it was like we could take up a conversation as if we were never apart. Even though we have only spoken by telephone a few times since those many years ago, I don't think we would have a problem striking up a lively conversation. He recently e-mailed some pictures from our days over there, validating that, yes, I was once young. I am proud to include some of those photos in this book.

I feel fortunate in that I do not think I have had significant posttraumatic stress issues. This is not to say that I have somehow pushed my experiences in Vietnam out of my mind. Obviously I have not, and I recognize this fact in a positive manner as much as possible. I admit that on the Fourth of July, when the large fireworks explode loudly, I think of those days in Vietnam, because some of them sound to me very similar to artillery and small-arms firefights. I don't have flashbacks or drop to the ground, but when they go off, I do give pause and experience a passing reflection of battles long ago. I recently read that this reaction to fireworks is a serious problem for some veterans even after all this time.

There is no doubt in my mind that part of the healing process that went on post-Vietnam in my case was that I met Joann, now my wonderful wife of nearly fifty years, while I was in college. She hails from Omaha, Nebraska, and that makes me a very lucky man to have taken summer jobs in the Big O back then. We've been blessed with three great children—a son and two daughters—along with our little pride-and-joy grandsons. I thank God that the draft was not going on by the time my son was of age to be drafted, and I hope with all of my heart that there is no need to reinstate it by the time my grandsons are of age. If we ever do have to reactivate the draft, the nation should administer it in a more impartial way than in the past, especially regarding deferments and other perceived special treatment.

I conclude now by saying that it my intent was to present the reader with verbal images and impressions of what one young man's experiences were like as he went from the peaceful confines of Kansas and Nebraska to the war-torn fields of South Vietnam. I deliberately focused on the broad range and depth of the feelings and emotions of war, not the weaponry or tactics of battle. I'm no expert in these later subjects, but I do have a deep appreciation for what I felt at that time in my life. I

14.1 Even though I was out of the service (active duty), when Mother asks you to take a picture in your Marine Corps uniform, you do it. I was an old man of twenty-two. Author's collection.

respectfully request that readers draw their own conclusions as to whether military personnel during the Vietnam War performed their duties up to past standards. Personally, I believe that we did our jobs in an honorable manner. I also believe that our senior military leaders had extremely complex duties that they carried out professionally and honorably. They did care about the safety of those under their command, and they did their best considering the task at hand. If veterans from past wars would have been with us physically, I know that they would have thought so, too.

EPILOGUE

Final Impressions

The one thing as certain as anything else from my days in South Vietnam is that no one has the ability to predict how a person will react when involved in combat situations. I've had the opportunity to gauge this behavioral response many times, daring for a moment to believe that I could foresee how someone might behave. The truth is that I didn't even know how I would respond to varying degrees of stress, particularly when people were doing their utmost to harm us. Age didn't matter, or should I say couldn't matter, because it had already been determined that seventeen years was old enough to put it all on the line.

No amount of training could have prepared us for the encounters that war brings, nor can it begin to retract the ligaments of the mind that have been emotionally stretched and repeatedly yanked near breaking-point extremes. Most of my patients never cried out in pain when they had every reason in the world to scream in sheer agony. This was not because their physical pain was any less, but I offer the possibility that they had already cried out in silent reverence for all of the misery and horror they had the misfortune to experience.

Another very large group of people perhaps suffered the most and witnessed more than all the others. I ask the reader to reflect on the image found at Figure E.1. This photograph illustrates who likely under-

E.1 South Vietnamese civilians among the survivors at Dong Xoai. Only a few of the several hundred civilians who sought refuge at the Dong Xoai post survived. Permission granted by AP photo, Horst Faas.

goes the most suffering in any war: the civilians who are many times caught squarely between those doing the fighting or who find themselves on the receiving end of intimidation or terroristic acts designed to capture their allegiance. This particular photo is of a Vietnamese family whose village of Dong Xoai fifty-five miles north of Saigon was attacked by some two thousand Viet Cong insurgents shortly after midnight one fateful night. The four hundred defenders within the village were overrun within an hour. Vietnamese Rangers were brought in by helicopter the next morning, and together with the Americans, Vietnamese Popular Forces, and the villagers themselves, the coalition eventually reclaimed the village many hours later after intense fighting.

This photograph was published in the July 2, 1965, issue of *LIFE* magazine. According to its accompanying article the image portrays a family that had been separated from one another during the fighting. They were no doubt driven into the surrounding countryside out of fear for their lives. Now they stood together crying in hysterical wonder that they all survived the attack and could be together after the eventual retaking of their village. All of their emotions were drawn together, yet there would be no rest for their weary bodies.

Numerous other images from that battle demonstrate in graphic detail the carnage that took place. Even though my unit wasn't there, it doesn't take much to imagine what went on that night. Twenty-one Americans did not have to imagine what happened, for they were among the dead, wounded, or missing after the battle. Regrettably we can apply the facial expressions in this picture to any number of nationalities in today's world. It matters little what nations they represent, for today's world has no shortage of refugees or war-torn countries.

These people had no weapons, no defense, and certainly no choice but to suffer within the state of affairs in which they found themselves. Neither age nor gender offered them any protection, for even if they were not directly targeted, they often became collateral damage. Think for a moment about some of the things that the grandmother in the picture has endured during her lifetime and all of the fear she has had to overcome awaiting the dawn of a new day. Look at her face. She bears emotional and physical scars from countless violent acts. What kinds of stories could she tell? Would the children in the photo ever be able to lead normal lives after the smell of gunpowder has long dissipated?

To make matters worse, these people probably suffered even longer after we left for home. Not only did they have to deal with a new government and all that it brought, but they also had to live with the aftereffects of the defoliant referred to as Agent Orange that was sprayed over vast areas of the countryside. Agent Orange was contaminated with a dioxin compound that led to death, birth defects, and serious medical problems for the Vietnamese people as well as our own military veterans. Volumes have been written about the use of this herbicide in Vietnam. The aim was to defoliate vegetation, thus exposing enemy trails and camps. In addition, the chemical was used to spray crops, which supposedly would reduce the insurgents' food supply. Neither of these objectives is a new concept in warfare strategy.

The objective of spraying Agent Orange certainly was not to kill or maim people directly. Who knew what and when regarding the deadly contaminant is well beyond the scope of this book or the knowledge of its author, but a great deal of information on this subject is available for those wishing to know more. Any veteran who was stationed in Vietnam or anywhere Agent Orange was stored, shipped, or handled should follow up with the Office of Veterans Affairs. The US government now recognizes many medical conditions as possibly being connected to the use of Agent Orange.

I would like to claim that while I was in Vietnam, I thought daily about what the civilians were going through, but I did not. Because of the nature of our relationships with the Vietnamese people, having mutual trust was difficult. Not only were some of them our enemy, but we could ill afford to open ourselves up for an unexpected betrayal of friendship. By and large we maintained a nonhostile, yet less personal approach, except for helping them in times of distress and the occasional goodwill visits. I am sure that most of us felt at some points a strong sense of empathy for those who by all indications were trying their utmost to eke out a living under extremely difficult circumstances in a very impoverished country. One of the most important reasons we were in their country was to help them survive the onslaught of an oppressive communist influence. We were fighting for their lives.

We all are allowed and in fact expected to share this special planet. I do not believe that we are equipped to know much more than this. People who believe that they have some sort of influence, real or imagined, on the rest of us might do well to reconsider their options. I am not aware of any other place for all humans to live together, and even if there were, we don't know how to get there alive. We can decide to live on this planet as one or to tear ourselves apart. The choice is ours.

INDEX

Page numbers in *italics* refer to figures.